TROUBLE IN EDEN

TROUBLE IN EDEN

A Comparison of the British and Swedish Economies

Eli Schwartz

PRAEGER

PRAEGER SPECIAL STUDIES • PRAEGER SCIENTIFIC

Library of Congress Cataloging in Publication Data

Schwartz, Eli.
   Trouble in Eden.

   Bibliography: p.
   Includes index.
   1. Great Britain--Economic policy--1945-
2. Sweden--Economic policy. 3. Sweden--Economic
conditions--1945-   4. Comparative economics.
I. Title.
HC256.5.S34   330.941'0857   80-17073
ISBN 0-03-057032-8

Published in 1980 by Praeger Publishers
CBS Educational and Professional Publishing
A Division of CBS, Inc.
521 Fifth Avenue, New York, New York 10017 U.S.A.

© 1980 by Praeger Publishers

0123456789   145   987654321

Printed in the United States of America

To the memory of Ehud Haim,
Haifa, Israel—A great intellectual companion.

Foreword by
Milton Friedman

In the immediate post-World War II period, history threw up an important economic and social experiment: the adoption of egalitarian socialist policies in Britain, and of what Ludwig Erhard called the "social market economy," in Germany. The experiment was biased in favor of Britain. Not only was Britain one of the victors and Germany a defeated country, but before the war, Britain had had a decidedly higher per-capita real income than Germany. In addition, Germany suffered far greater destruction of its productive capacity, its housing, its public amenities (what have come inelegantly to be called infrastructure). Consequently, if Britain had performed better in the postwar period than Germany, those of us who believe, on moral and ethical, and not merely economic, grounds, in a free market system would have had an out. We could have attributed the result to Britain's initial advantages.

As it happened, the outcome was clear-cut and unambiguous. As Professor Schwartz notes, by 1976, per-capita real output in Germany was roughly double that in the United Kingdom. The results strongly confirmed a view I repeatedly expressed in the early 1950s: if such an experiment had to be made, how much better it would have been for the political health of the world, if the roles had been reversed, if Germany had experimented with egalitarian socialism, and Britain, with a social market economy.

However, there has been one disturbing element in that interpretation of the experiment: Sweden. Here was a country which also adopted a policy of egalitarian socialism, yet flourished, experiencing a high rate of growth, and attaining high levels of living for its population. How come?

That is the question Eli Schwartz addresses in this book. His examination of the British experience illuminates our understanding of what went wrong, and of what changes are needed if Britain is to meet the objectives of its citizens. It also provides a benchmark for judging a new experiment that may be unfolding: Margaret Thatcher's determination to widen the scope of the market, to reverse highly egalitarian policies, and establish a framework that will encourage rapid growth.

Professor Schwartz's examination of the Swedish experience is equally valuable in removing some of the mystery about its success. It turns out that Sweden is now experiencing many of the difficulties that have plagued Britain for a longer period. Growth has slowed down sharply in recent years; there is widespread dissatisfaction with governmental tax, spending, and industrial policies; and current economic difficulties appear not to be simply a temporary aberration, but a harbinger of further troubles yet to come. The puzzle is not success versus failure, but the more limited question of why the basic forces took so much longer to show up in Sweden than in Britain.

Professor Schwartz's answer is multiple: partly, egalitarian redistributive policies were initially less drastic after World War II in Sweden than in the United Kingdom, and then accelerated more rapidly, so that they are now more drastic, and the later growth meant the later emergence of serious problems; partly, the greater homogeneity of the Swedish than of the British population reduced frictions and fostered pragmatic and realistic agreement; partly, the greater openness of Sweden to international trade enabled competition abroad to discipline governmental control at home.

We in the United States, as we proceed along the British road, and increasingly encounter the same problems, can benefit greatly from this calm, serious, informed examination of an important economic and social experiment.

INTRODUCTION

Compared to the other Western European economies, the British have not done well in the postwar period. This has been often ascribed to the socialist direction of the British economy. On the other hand, the Swedes (who also profess to a socialist economy) have done quite well—at least until quite recently.

I have thought that an unravelling of some of the factors behind this puzzle might prove interesting. My desire has been to write a book consisting of a comparative study of the economies of the United Kingdom and Sweden against the backdrop of developments in the other Western economies. The purpose would be to analyze some of the factors that have inhibited the United Kingdom from achieving a satisfactory rate of economic progress and to uncover some of the factors behind the relative success of the Swedish economy. The broader goal was an attempt to convert the lessons learned into economic-policy recommendations.

To gain a perspective on the relative success and failures of the British and Swedish economies, I read widely in newspapers, periodicals, and books. In the spring and summer of 1978, I traveled to Sweden and made my third trip to England. I spoke to various businessmen, academics, and journalists in both countries in order to gain some perspective on economic developments and policies.

My interviewees are not to be blamed for all the opinions in this book. The intention of the book is to be provocative (in the sense of inducing critical thought), and for this I take the major responsibility. The point of view is fairly clear. It is not that the market system performs all economic functions perfectly, but it does do better than a directed economy in solving a large number of problems. (Many difficult aspects of our own society, which some are too prone to blame on the workings of a capitalistic system, arise out of inherent conflicts of values, or are derived from human failings, and would not disappear in a socialistic system.) At any rate, in the cases of Sweden and Great Britain, the reasoned conclusion of my study is that too many resources are being devoted to the nonmarket sector (allocated by bureaucrats) or are passed along by transfer of incomes to allow for maximum economic efficiency. My research has led me to believe that both economies would do better if, at this point, the social sector were reduced or at least restrained, and the private-market sector allowed some relative growth.

It is perhaps unfortunate that all the Western economies are currently experiencing considerable external stress, so that any present implementation of policies favorable to the market sector may not receive the fairest of tests. It is all too possible that many observers will place the onus for the difficulties the Western economies are presently experiencing on the implementation of more realistic domestic economic policies, when perhaps the real problems are the result of unsettled conditions in the third world. Nevertheless, the change of policy direction and philosophy toward more individual responsibility and incentive does hold some hope for the future.

For our own country, the import of this study is quite clear. On parallel paths, we have been moving in much the same direction as the United Kingdom and Sweden. We too must slow the growth of the governmental and redistributional sector, before we find it in control of 50 to 65 percent of the gross national product, and we find ourselves wrestling with the economic frictions and constraints such a development will bring.

It is only fitting that I acknowledge as much as possible the help and encouragement I received in writing this book. There are all my colleagues at Lehigh, especially Finn Jensen, and two patient secretaries, Mrs. Esther Judd and Mrs. Patricia Wendling, and my student assistants Barry Levine and Miles Berkow. Other helpers in the United States included Joel Segall, Jack Guttentag, Aron Katsenelinboigen, and Milton Friedman. In Sweden, the people who graciously spent some time with me include Franz Ettlin, Karl Gustaf Jungenfelt, David Laidler, Eric Lundberg, all at the Stockholm Graduate School of Business (Handel Höch-Schule); Jan Bröms of the Federation of Swedish Industries; Robert Sherwood, economic affairs, American Embassy; Walter Frankel, businessman; and most helpfully, Ölle Lindgren of the Skandinaviska Enskilda Banken. In England, the following were very helpful: Karl Klapholz, Lord Robbins, and Peter Wiles of the London School of Economics; Robert Bacon, Walter Eltis, and Morris Scott of Oxford University; E. E. Nelson of Lloyds; Donald Silk of the City of London; Alex Clayman, London; Chris Foster and Robert Gifford of York University; Samuel Brittan of the Financial Times; and Andrew Gottschalk of the London Graduate School of Business.

I should acknowledge the help of Alan G. Schwartz, who accompanied me on many of my interviews and gave me aid and encouragement, and that of Paul Joseph, who read and commented on early versions of the manuscript.

I should like to thank all the librarians who put up with my nagging.

I am grateful to the Earhart Foundation for supporting my research.

CONTENTS

TROUBLE IN EDEN

1

THE BRITISH RETARDATION

THE CHANGE IN RELATIVE INCOME LEVELS

The post-World War II period has been one of mostly sustained growth for the developed economies. Nevertheless, some countries have been more successful than others. Germany, whose per-capita income was about 50 percent of that of the United States in the 1930s, has now reached a level of real GNP per capita that is close to that of the United States. France lags only slightly behind. However, the United Kingdom, which started out with a relative per-capita income of 64 percent of the United States in the 1950s, is now down to a level of about 43 percent.

Table 1.1 gives us some comparative per capita GNP data, in U. S. dollars, for France, Germany, Sweden, the United Kingdom, and the United States, from 1950 to 1976. We do not vouch for the exact economic comparability of all these figures. In the later years, they are largely based on exchange-rate translations. They do not account for the differences in the prices for internal goods to various countries, nor do they account for the fact that when internal prices differ and national tastes differ, the market basket of goods will vary between countries. (This is a problem inherent in all index-number constructions.) Moreover, the figures represent per-capita gross national products; as such, they do not account for the amount of leisure taken, for household-produced services, and for external diseconomies, such as the amount of pollution not counted in the costs of production. They do not account for the fact that in some countries, relatively more of the GNP may be used for national defense or, necessarily, for crime detection and prevention. (Of course, over time, these will influence reported income, since a relatively heavy rate of expenditures in these areas can reduce

1

TABLE 1.1

Per-Capita GNP in Dollars

Country	1950	1955	1965	1973	1976
France	968	1,285	2,047	4,851	6,700
Germany	782	1,333	1,939	5,618	7,000
Sweden	1,190	1,577	2,713	6,155	8,500
United Kingdom	1,133	1,470	1,870	3,120	3,360
United States	1,830	2,310	3,580	6,155	7,830

Source: From 1965 on, the data are from the OECD national accounts, simply converted by the exchange rate. The data for 1950 and 1955 use U.S. price weights and are from Milton Gilbert and Associates, Comparative National Products and Price Levels (Paris: OEEC, 1958). The 1950 and 1955 data for Sweden have been estimated by adjusting the Yang relatives (see J. H. Yang, "Comparing Per Capita Output Internationally: Has the United States Been Overtaken?" Federal Reserve Bank of St. Louis Review, May 1978) to the Gilbert data for the other countries.

capital formation and result in a lower growth rate.) Lastly, different sources for the data, and different methods of converting figures into reasonable common monetary denominators, can give different measures for the value of the national GNPs.

All these provisos must be taken into consideration in making fine distinctions; however, they need not worry us in the present case. Alternative measures of relative per-capita output are shown in Table 1.2. In this table, J. H. Yang has made an attempt to get beyond the simple exchange-rate translation, by constructing a purchasing-power index based both on the prices of internationally traded goods and on domestic goods. [1] Under this method of comparison, the present U.S. GNP per capita is still significantly ahead of that of the other countries. Nevertheless, the general trend still shows that Sweden, Germany, and France significantly narrowed the gap between their output and that of the United States during the postwar period, whereas the United Kingdom has about the same relative position it had in 1950.

Thus, all observers report consistent trends for the growth of these countries' per capita GNPs, although the absolute differences and the rankings vary somewhat. The data are sufficient for our purposes.

The United Kingdom is obviously the failure among Western European economies. This is ascribed to a multitude of factors; prominent among them is an overdose of socialism. However, Sweden, which had a semisocialist system from the 1930s up until 1976, had a real rate of growth in excess of that of the United States in the 1950-76 period, although somewhat below that of Western Europe. In 1976, as reported by the World Bank, assuming the official monetary exchange rate, the per-capita income of Sweden in 1976 was slightly ahead of that of the United States. (Of course, the reporting on Sweden has tended, up until recently, to be exaggeratedly favorable; a careful follower of events will know that Sweden is not without its social and economic tensions. Moreover, the economic problems intensified in 1977, 1978, and 1979.) In fact Sweden has had no perceptible real growth in the last few years.

The questions that we wish to explore are twofold. Using Sweden and Great Britain as a base of comparison, can one identify the strategic factors that inhibited England from achieving a satisfactory rate of economic progress in the postwar period? And secondly, is it possible to uncover the unfavorable factors that have impinged on the Swedish economy in the last three years, eliciting a state of

TABLE 1.2

International Comparisons of Per-Capita Output, Based on Purchasing-Power Parities, 1950, 1960, 1970, 1974, and 1976 (United States = 100)

Country	1950	1960	1970	1974	1976
United States	100	100	100	100	100
France	46	58	75	81	NA*
Germany	37	64	75	76	76
Sweden	58	69	78	78	77
United Kingdom	55	64	60	61	59

*Not available.

Source: J.-H. Yang, "Comparing Per Capita Output Internationally: Has the United States Been Overtaken?" Federal Reserve Bank of St. Louis Review, May 1978.

malaise and discouragement among Swedish economists and business-men?

EXPLAINING DIFFERENTIAL GROWTH RATES—
THE CATCHUP PHASE

In order to isolate the factors making for different national income levels and rates of growth, some guidelines from economic theory would be useful. Under orthodox theory, where countries have approximately similar political-social structures and a similar quality of education and skills among the population, income levels are set by the proportion of the other productive factors—capital and natural resources—to labor. According to the law of proportionality, the marginal product of each factor depends on the relative supply of the other factors. Thus, in a country where labor is relatively scarce, compared to an abundance of land and capital, the marginal product and income of labor would be high. (Moreover, the per-capita income in such a country is high since the aggregate return to capital and land is counted in the numerator, i. e. , total national income; but the supply of these factors does not affect the denominator, i. e. , the total population.) In another situation, where there is a relatively large supply of quality labor, but capital is relatively scarce, the marginal productivity of capital and its return should be relatively high.

However, what we have been discussing are essentially closed and static models. What happens if we allow for some migration of factors, international trade, or economic growth? The general economic understanding is that both trade and migration lead toward the equalization of factor incomes and are somewhat substitutable for each other. However, it is quite probable that the process of economic growth also tends toward the equalization of factor incomes.

In the first case, where we allow for the migration of factors, the mobile factors, labor and capital, would tend to move to those areas where they have a relatively better return. Except for some degree of economic immobility—human reluctance to move or to risk capital in other countries—the returns to the factors of equal quality in all regions should equalize.

In the second case, if trade opens up between two regions having disproportionate mixes of factors, the regions will mainly sell to each other those products which embody the output of their relatively abundant factors. This would raise the rate of return of the abundant factors and lower the rate of return of the scarce factors, in each country. According to a very intriguing demonstration by P. A. Samuelson and W. F. Stolper, under conditions of free trade in goods, the factors would be employed in the same combinations in each industry, in each country, and the return to the factors in each country would be exactly equal except for transport costs and other frictions. [2] However, there is some doubt that complete equalization will be achieved, even under static conditions, if one posits, first, a substantial amount of natural resources, varying both in quantity and quality, in the two countries or regions; and second, a significant amount of domestic industries, whose output does not enter into trade but is consumed domestically.

The first two forces, migration and trade, have long been discussed in economic literature, and their effect on factor-price equality is fairly clear. What we may also note is that income inequality, which is the result of a disequilibrium situation, can also be corrected by differential rates of economic growth. Quite simply, if, due to war or other instances of prolonged economic upset, the capital stock of a country has been stunted relative to other comparable areas, the productivity of capital investment in the curtailed area will be relatively high. This means there will be a high profit rate, and a strong incentive to invest in real capital. This should bring about a high rate of capital formation and a relatively high rate of economic growth. Gross output will increase as the new capacity comes on stream.

The returns to capital in the formerly repressed area will be relatively high. The desired capital investments can be financed by foreign sources, or by voluntary domestic savings encouraged by the prevailing high rate of return, or by involuntary savings—credit creation and price inflation—or by some combination of all three. (According to the value judgment of most economists, the less of the third, the better.)

In the long run, the increased amount of real capital will eventually bring down the marginal rate of return on capital to that prevailing in other areas—allowing, of course, for any residual frictions and factor quality differentials. At this point, the rate of growth in the once-temporarily capital-short country should slow to that of other countries with similar-quality labor forces and managerial skills.

This analysis, which rests within the framework of orthodox economic theory, can account for a large part of observed economic growth as differential growth—i. e., the catching up an economically regressed area. What the analysis does not contain are the explanations for the economic growth of the lead areas. Presumably, this must rest on such factors as the rate of the discovery and implementation of innovations, and the deepening of the capital stock. [3]

Given the ground rules of the neoclassical model, the postwar economic miracle of West Germany, for example, is not quite so astounding. A tremendous amount of capital had been destroyed during the war. Per-capita output in Germany in 1950 was below that of France and of the United Kingdom, and whereas by 1950 France and the United Kingdom had surpassed their prewar output, Germany was still significantly below the level achieved in 1938. Thus, if 1938 output is set at the base, 100, the index for industrial production for the United Kingdom in 1950 was 127; for France, 122; and for West Germany, 93.5.[4] The same factor, a past retardation of capital formation, would account for the fact that the growth rate in Western Europe as a whole has exceeded that of the United States in the postwar period. Moreover, by about 1960, once there had been some catching up between West Germany and France, the growth of these two countries moved at a more even pace. Thus, according to the World Bank, the per-capita income growth of France was 4.2 percent per annum from 1960 to 1975, compared to 3.5 percent for Germany. The absolute level of the two countries' income on an exchange-rate basis is only insignificantly higher in favor of Germany.

To sum up, economic analysis suggests that in countries of roughly similar cultural and social development, as long as any large element of open market exists, relative rates of economic growth should be mainly determined by strong real forces. High rates of growth for a repressed country can be largely explained, by economic theory, as a form of adjustment to a disequilibrium situation. Of course, as is true of most economic theorems, the adjustments predicted by the model are not instantaneous and not precisely correct under all conditions; nevertheless the analysis is predictive and useful in analyzing trends. No one in possession of this bit of economic reasoning should have been surprised by the rapid rate of growth of the Western European economies, nor at the narrowing of the gap between these countries and the United States in the postwar period. In the not-so-long run, therefore, the Western European economies should have caught up with the British early postwar lead. However, the mystery remains; there is no fundamental economic reason why the other Western European countries should have thereafter passed England by such a wide margin.

COMPARATIVE INCOME LEVELS, INSTITUTIONAL ARRANGEMENTS, AND POLICY DIRECTIONS

As has been noted, there are several factors which might preclude the complete working out of the equal-income hypothesis. We might classify these as, first, inherent variables, such as significan differences in the technical skills and quality of the labor force (where immigration is restricted), and/or a disparity in the natural-resource endowment: the amount and fertility of arable land, and the amount of coal deposits, oil, and other mineral resources per capita. Second, we might note noninherent factors, i.e. , the existence of policies and institutions that inhibit economic efficiency and rationality.

Regarding its inherent variables the Swedes probably have a somewhat better resource base than do the British, but it is hardly of an amount sufficient to explain the existing disparity where the Swedes have 2.5 times the GNP per capita of the British. Moreover, if natural-resource endowment were the vital factor, we should still need to explain why West Germany (a country whose resource base is not spectacular) has a current GNP per capita that is two times that of the British. Since the quality of the British population is probably equal to that of the rest of Western Europe, and since there are no singular differences in resources, the likely conclusion is that the disparity in growth rates is mainly due to the restrictive institutional arrangements, and to the inhibiting effect of the economic policies pursued by the British in the postwar period.

The underlying motif of British policy since the war has been the drive for equality or fair shares; this has been given priority over considerations of economic efficiency or of economic growth. The leitmotif policy stems from an inordinate fear of unemployment, which has made the shifting of economic resources very difficult, and which has resulted in a swift progression of public-employment jobs. In actual practice, the prevailing philosophy brought about a premature postwar provision of a high level of public services, which reduced the funds available for industrial capital, and which, combined with the prevailing left-wing fear of profits, has dampened the level of investment. It is argued that the high marginal levels of taxation, aggressive unionism, and restrictive labor practices have worked to restrain individual incentives. The remnants of the empire-preference system, and the failure to join the European Common Market at its inception, blunted the discipline of competition.

Of course, one may argue that economic equality (if it can be defined) is its own reward. The absolute level of the income shares is not as important as the equality of the division. One may rationally argue in favor of what Arthur Okun describes as the "leaky-bucket theorem," which holds that the transfer of income from the rich to the poor is worthwhile even if some wealth is lost in the process. [5] However, as Okun points out, how much one may be willing to lose in the redistribution process, before calling a halt, is a judgmental matter. There is a considerable opinion, in England, that redistribution through the use of the government fisc has gone far enough. [6]

At any rate, there are at least two problems with redistribution that the bloodless world of economic description tends to miss. The first is that many people who make a higher income seem to really

TABLE 1. 3

Life Expectancies, Selected Countries, 1975

Country	Average Life Expectancy in Years	
	Men	Women
Sweden	72. 1	77. 7
Norway	71. 2	77. 4
Denmark	70. 7	76. 1
Finland	65. 9	74. 2
Federal Republic of Germany	67. 4	73. 8
United Kingdom	68. 9	75. 1
France	68. 6	76. 4
Italy	69. 0	74. 9
Netherlands	71. 2	77. 2
Belgium	67. 8	74. 2
Switzerland	70. 2	76. 2
United States	67. 4	75. 1
Japan	70. 5	75. 9
Average	69. 3	75. 7

Source: World Health Organization, cited in The United Kingdom in 1980: the Hudson Report, New York, John Wiley & Sons, 1974.

believe that they deserve it, on the basis of such factors as superior talent, energy, training, or length of loyal service. Many of these people might like to contribute to a voluntary charity, but at the same time, will resent a heavy differential tax burden as not being quite just. (It might be noted that many Western European societies discourage private charity, considering it somehow a subversion of socialist morality.)[7] Not many scholars have seriously studied the question of whether a flat-income system would make a group more content than a system which offers differential rewards. (If in practice, a particular trade union does opt for a flat standard among its members, one may still note the vigor with which the union fights to keep any differential over less deserving groups.) The second drawback to massive redistributive policies may be their negative effect on the morale and morality of the recipients themselves. Apparently, the receivers of some benefit programs show signs of social debilitation. In short, no one can show that a strong program of income equalization makes for a totally happier society.

If on the basis of the leaky-bucket theorem, the British economy has traded some growth for more equal income redistribution, it is not clear that the result has been a net gain in the sum total of human happiness. On the basis of objective data, the authors of the Hudson Report concluded that the quality of life in England presently is not significantly better than that in the countries of Western Europe (which some British commentators like to think of as somehow more competitive and less humane). In fact, infant-mortality rates are a commendable 16 per 1,000 in England, but they are only 14 per 1,000 in France, and 11 per 1,000 in Switzerland and in the Netherlands. [8] Data (see Table 1.3) for 1975 show that life expectancy of males in England is 68.9 years, about average for the list of developed countries. Life expectancy for females is 75.1 years, also about at the average. At any rate, the point of the Hudson Report was that, whereas in 1950 the United Kingdom led all these countries except the Netherlands in these statistics, today the differences are hardly noticeable.

THE "LUMP-OF-LABOR" THEORY OF EMPLOYMENT

The drive for equality, no matter the cost in economic efficiency, has in practice been combined with a pervading fear of unemployment. At the higher levels of policy making, this has led to the use of the Keynesian fiscal instruments or demand management policies to ensure full employment; at the operational level of union practices, it has led to overmanning, resistance to innovations, and a slowdown in labor productivity. On a basic level the worker tends to believe in the "lump-of-labor" theory of employment: that there is only so much work to go around; that if the workers work too hard or too efficiently, they will soon work themselves out of a job. This attitude is, by no means, confined to England. However, in England it seems to have been implemented as actual behavior more than it has elsewhere. [9]

The difficulty of ridding people of the lump-of-labor illusion rests on the fact that at the microlevel, it appears to be true. Thus, if in a given industry, people are forced to retire early, it seems that more jobs will be available for new entrants into the labor force. However, if the workers were willing and able to work longer, the older workers would then earn a current income. This income would be counted in total demand and be available to buy the output of the new workers (who also would have an income to buy products). In short, the equilibrium amount of aggregate demand should suffice to employ the full labor force (including older people) willing to work.

(Essentially, we have a modified Say's Law; there cannot be a generalized oversupply of labor; only, on occasion, a shortage of aggregate demand.) The cure for a temporary or disequilibrium shortfall of aggregate demand can hardly rest in such remedies as early retirement, or restrictive employment practices. In fact, these are only methods of sharing the unemployment.

As to the singular problems that a socialist government would face with the English unions, we refer to Joseph Schumpeter:

> But the real problem is labor. Unless socialization is spell economic breakdown, a socializing government cannot possibly tolerate present trade-union practice. The most irresponsible of politicians would, in the case envisaged, have to face the basic problem of modern society that only Russia has solved, the problem of industrial discipline. A government that means to socialize to any great extent will have to socialize trade unions. And, as things actually are, labor is of all things the most difficult to socialize. Not that the problem is insoluble. In England, the chances for successful solution by the political method of democracy are greater than they are anywhere else. But the road to solution may be tortuous and long. [10]

It should not be thought that the Keynesian economists (a group with considerable brainpower) overlooked the problems of union power and labor restrictions in the dampening of the level of output and economic growth. However, they are optimistic that a long period of sustained full employment would dissipate the workers' fears and lead to an abatement of featherbedding policies. In the actual course of events, the postwar record on unemployment was better than most had hoped for; nevertheless, it has done very little to erode labor attitudes in favor of defensive make-work rules. (Robbins remarks that Keynes's prescription was correct for the 1930s. He also notes that Keynes thought that if unemployment was reduced to 500,000 (about 4 percent of the labor force), problems of full employment would reassert themselves. Unemployment in postwar England has been well below this figure until recently.)[11]

THE HANDICAP OF OLD CAPITAL

There is a line of popular thought which holds that the defeated countries were able to grow during the postwar period because they were not burdened with old and obsolete capital, as was England.

This is an argument which is hard for an economist to fathom, because it implies that nothing is better than something. However, T. H. White may have hit on an element of truth when he wrote on the American postwar policies toward Great Britain and West Germany. White ascribed the significant causative factor in the divergent growth of the two countries not to the amount of age of their capital stock, but to the psychology of work and the deferral of expectations inculcated into the German economic psychology:

> The Law of Unintended Consequences is what twists history's chronology into drama. Our treatment of England and Germany is a classic example of the Law's operation. After victory we began by seeking to punish the Germans for Hitler's savageries and to help the British for having defended freedom's way for all people. We ended, by the logic of the Marshall Plan and the Law of Unintended Consequences, in dismissing from greatness the British, our allies, and elevating the Germans, our enemies, to the status of Europe's senior power. . . .
>
> The result, thirty years later, is amusing to consider. I first stumbled on its roots in a conversation with one of Lucius Clay's economic experts. . . . Clay's expert was quite simple. "Our policy," he said, "is to make these bastards work their way back." The Germans should be forced to work, and work hard, he felt, to pay for the food, fiber and raw material that American humanitarians believed we must ship in via the Marshall Plan.
>
> Other West European governments were democratic governments; as all modern elected governments must, they promised more—more good houses, more schools, more health insurance, more equality. The most democratic and responsible government in Europe was the British government; it promised its people most. The most autocratic government in Europe was West Germany—and its autocrat was the U. S. Army. England, France, Belgium had governments that could vote on how many hours went into a working week, and what maternity benefits should be, and how many days or weeks of vacation people should have. In Germany, Lucius Clay and his advisors decided that Germans must work a 48-hour week, and work they did. The U. S. Army said the Germans must rebuild their factories, roads and bridges first; meanwhile, let them shiver in cellars, ruins and rags; no housing or clothing until they earned their way back.

It was years before I could fully measure the results
of the Law of Unintended Consequences. When I first reported Europe, shortly after the war, the British standard
of living was roughly three times that in refugee-crammed
West Germany. Since then, somehow, England has gone
its jovial way across its pleasant plateau of civility, but
Germany has boomed. The average per capita income in
victorious England had risen to $3,871 thirty years later—
while in defeated Germany it had reached $7,336, and the
gap was widening. Somehow, the severity with which the
Americans policed Germany and directed the flow of aid
proved more fruitful than the affection and support we
gave the free government of the English people to do as
they wished with our billions. [12]

Of course, White, as is even true of good journalists, tends to
exaggerate. The Benelux countries and France, which received sym-
pathy and U.S. aid, also outdid England in the postwar period. (But
in a certain sense, these were also defeated countries where the
population understood that they would have to work themselves back
to recovery.)

WHAT OF SWEDEN?

However, lastly, we have the case of Sweden, which came out
of the war with most of its capital and institutional arrangements
intact; moreover, Sweden also had a social-democratic government
presumably intent on giving its citizens a hearty dose of welfare.
Let us say, at this point, that it is easier to discuss or explain
the slowdown of the British economy than to explain the relative success of the Swedes. But before we detail some of the developments
in the two economies, we should note that the Swedish economy, as
of the last few years, has not shown any real growth, and that among
Swedish businessmen and economists, there is a growing uneasiness
over the lack of growth, the drop in profitability, the rise in company
failures, and the present high level of unemployment (overt and concealed). At any rate, the Swedes tend to cite three factors which
could explain the relative success of the Swedish economy (up until
recently): the openness of the economy to foreign competition; the
relative reasonableness of labor as long as the economy was growing,
and, possibly, the existence of a natural-resource base, in the form
of timber and iron ore, which provided some natural rents or surpluses. The latter could be distributed without distorting economic
efficiency too grievously. (Karl-Gustaf Jungenfelt thought the expla-

nation for the Swedish success might be that the Swedes experienced good outcomes on risky investments; in other words, the Swedes were lucky in making capital investments in the postwar period. However, the main Swedish industries, steel, shipbuilding, and autos, are surprisingly similar to those of the United Kingdom.) Another recurring theme implied simply that the socialist redistribution policies had rested rather lightly on the economy in the first 25 years of the postwar period, and that their strangulating effect was only now being felt as the creature grew into its collar.

NOTES

1. J. H. Yang, "Comparing Per Capita Output Internationally: Has the United States Been Overtaken?" Federal Reserve Bank of St. Louis Review, May 1978. The pioneering work for this kind of measure was done by M. Gilbert and I. Kravis, An International Comparison of National Products and the Purchasing Power of Currencies (Paris: OEEC, 1954).

2. Wolfgang F. Stolper and Paul Samuelson, "Protection and Real Wages," The Review of Economic Studies 9 (1941/42). Reprinted in Readings in the Theory of International Trade (Blakiston: American Economics Association, 1949).

3. Much of the foregoing argument can be found in E. Schwartz, "On Relative Rates of Economic Growth," Weltwirtschaftliches Archiv, Spring 1964.

4. General Statistics (OEEC) 6 (1954): 7.

5. Arthur M. Okun, Equality and Efficiency: The Big Tradeoff (Washington, D.C.: Brookings Institution, 1975).

6. For a popular version of this opinion, see Patrick Hutber, The Decline and Fall of the Middle Class (Harmondsworth: Penguin Books, 1976).

7. New York Times, July 2, 1978, p. 1.

8. The United Kingdom in 1980: the Hudson Report (New York: Wiley, 1974); also, New York Times, June 6, 1978, p. 2.

9. Among others, see Lord Robbins, Aspects of the Post-War Economic Policy (London: Institute of Economic Affairs, 1974).

10. Joseph A. Schumpeter, Capitalism, Socialism, and Democracy (New York: Harper Bros., 1947), p. 379.

11. Robbins, op. cit.

12. T. H. White, In Search of History (New York: Harper and Row, 1978).

2

A FAILURE OF NERVE:
GREAT BRITAIN AFTER 1945

About the turn of the century, the United Kingdom began to lag behind the United States in output per capita. A rough comparison of the historic trends in the per-capita income of the two countries, in current dollars, is given in Table 2.1. The difference in per-capita income was probably not very great in the early years of the century. The gap widened to 26 percent during the 1920s but narrowed somewhat to 16 percent during the 1930s. The fact is that Great Britain weathered the depression relatively better than did the United States. The developments of the 1930s are explainable in terms of the relatively greater fall of income and the higher rate of increase in unemployment in the American economy, not in terms of an acceleration in British growth. Moreover, if we consider not realized output, but changes in potential output, there was considerable implicit growth in the American economy throughout the late 1930s. From about 1880 to 1900 Sweden lagged behind in per capita GDP. In the 1920s, Sweden caught up with England, but the United States drew ahead of them. From the mid-1940s to 1960, Sweden began to draw even with the United States and the United Kingdom fell progressively further behind.

THE IMMEDIATE POSTWAR SITUATION

But the major point in discussing English economic performance is that we are not dealing with an undeveloped country. At the end of World War II, England was ahead of the major countries of Europe in the supply of civil amenities (see Table 2.2). The United Kingdom came out of World War II with considerable real resources; among other items, she possessed a literate population, working

FIGURE 2.1

Trend of United States, Sweden, and England,
GDP per Capita, 1880-1980
(1979 Prices)

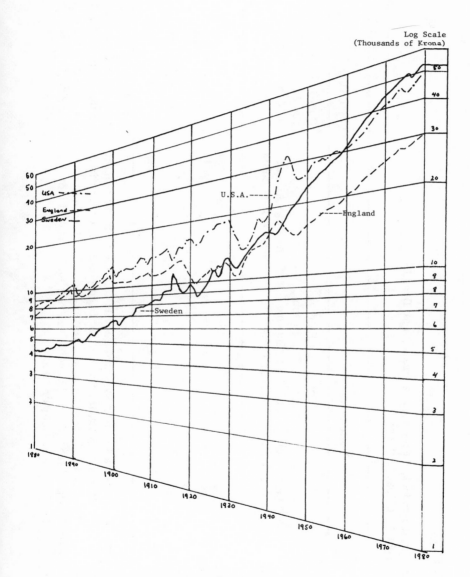

Source: Veckans affärer (October 1979).

TABLE 2.1

Net National Product, Per-Capita Average, Per Decade (in current American dollars)

	United States		United Kingdom		
Decade	Average Annual Income Per Capita	Compound Rate of Growth, Per Annum, of Money Income Per Capita	Average Annual Income Per Capita	Compound Rate of Growth, Per Annum, of Money Income Per Capita	Percentage of U.S. Income
1900–09	$244	–	$220	–	90%
1910–19	362	4.0%	336	4.3%	93
1920–29	636	5.8	469	3.4	74
1930–39	484	0	407	0	84
1940–49	877	6.1	685	5.3	78

Note: There are a few provisos that go with this table. In the original tables, the decades for the two countries were off by one year; the translation from pounds to dollars is made on the basis of the official exchange rate; the data are in current money terms and do not take into consideration price-level changes.

Source: Adapted from Simon Kuznets, "Levels and Variability of Rates of Growth," Economic Development and Cultural Change, October 1956.

TABLE 2.2

Some Indexes of the Supply of Consumer Capital—1937 Compared to 1948 and 1950 (per 1,000 population)

Country	Motor Vehicles		Telephones		Radios	
	1937	1948	1937	1948	1937	1950
Sweden	21.4	26.2	115.0	207.0	195.0	307.0
United Kingdom	38.8	40.34	64.0	97.0	181.0	244.0
France	49.0	37.25	37.0	55.0	114.0	165.0
Germany	16.0	4.6	53.0	15.3	169.0	180.0
United States	88.0	218.0	151.0	261.0	316.0	560.0

Source: United Nations, Statistical Year Book (New York, 1949–50).

TABLE 2. 3

Trend of U. K. Outstanding Sterling Balances, 1945-53

Year-End	Balance (billions of £)	As Percent of U. K. GNP
1945	2. 008	20. 3
1946	1. 924	19. 2
1947	1. 787	16. 5
1948	1. 809	15. 1
1949	1. 771	14. 0
1950	1. 980	14. 8
1951	1. 825	12. 4
1952	1. 606	10. 1
1953	1. 758	10. 3

Source: Judd Polk, Sterling: Its Meaning in World Finance (New York: Harper and Bros. , 1956, p. 163).

harbors, and a functioning internal transportation and communication network of cars and lorries, and telephones. Her capital equipment may have been old and somewhat deteriorated, having been heavily worked during the war, but the capital was nevertheless still largely in place. In fact, at the end of the war, the United Kingdom had no large intact industrial rival other than the United States.

Against her real assets must be placed the fact that, in order to finance the war effort, Britain had lost a great deal in the way of financial claims. Assets in the rest of the world, such as investments in the United States and Latin America, had been sold to pay for armaments and supplies. Moreover, postwar Britain had to face the overhang of the sterling balances. This represented money owed, on current account, to various sterling-bloc countries from which Great Britain had purchased supplies or services. As can be seen in Table 2. 3, the sterling balances in 1945 amounted to about $8 billion, 20 percent of the nominal GNP of approximately $40 billion.

Nevertheless, it is our contention that the positive real factors outweighed the financial liabilities. The intermediate-run situation after World War II favored the technologically advanced, capital-intensive countries. That Great Britain did not share fully in the postwar progress of these countries is due to social and governmental policies, and not to any inherent poverty of the British Isles.

LABOR'S UPSET WIN

In the 1945 postwar election, the British voted in a Labor government. The Labor-party victory was largely based on historic reasons. The Conservative government of Winston Churchill was surely not a failure in terms of organizing and mobilizing the economy for the war effort. However, what the voters seemed to recall was the end of World War I, when the election slogan had been "a country fit for heroes." As it turned out, the post-World War I economic adjustment was quite severe; unemployment went up to about 15. 0 percent in the 1921 recession and remained at about 11. 0 percent for the rest of the decade; the level of industrial output in 1922 dropped to 62 percent of the 1913 base and did not fully return to the 1913 level until 1929. The Labor party won the post-World War II election on the memory of the post-World War I recession. (This is not surprising; many think that the Democrats won the U. S. election of 1948 on the basis of the crash of 1929.)

In point of fact, the Laborites were shocked to find themselves winners. A book by C. A. R. Crosland noted:*

When the Labour Party took office in July 1945, it at once found itself confronted with an unexpected situation. It had had years, even decades, in which to familiarize itself and the country with the details of its traditional programme of socialist reform, and it had naturally assumed that this programme would command its undivided attention once in office. The depression of [the] 1930s had, it is true, shown the necessity for a short-term economic policy, and full employment took its place alongside social reform as a prime objective. But it was always thought that the Party would come to power during a slump, and that the monetary expansion required to combat depression would at once justify and facilitate the pursuit of the traditional objectives of equality and higher living standards. Economic and social policy would thus march hand in hand. [1]

---

*Crosland eventually held cabinet positions in a number of Labor governments. His book throws some light on the prevailing mood of the time. Its forecasts on world economic growth and potential were considerably on the short side of actual developments.

AN ANTIDEFLATIONARY POLICY

Essentially, then, the Labor party expected to find itself put
in charge of a mature (nongrowth) economy faced with a shortage of
aggregate demand. The remedies for such a situation were clearly
spelled out by Alvin H. Hansen. [2] (One must be fair to Hansen. His
remedies were probably appropriate to the disease; the question involves the important matter of diagnosis.) A deflationary situation
called for income redistribution, to raise the level of consumption
relative to savings (so that the level of savings would be appropriate
for a lower level of investment); it called for the provision of massive
measures of social security, so that the incentive for personal savings would be reduced; and for an increase of spending on public-
sector goods. Thus were social justice and economic good sense to
be combined.

But the situation at the end of the war was hardly deflationary.
The money supply had grown from a 1938 level of £2. 699 billion
(56. 1 percent of the national income) to a 1945 level of £5. 825 billion
(68. 7 percent of the national income), as seen in Table 2. 4. Goods
were generally in short supply; their prices had been controlled since
the start of the war, and there was a strongly enforced system of
rationing. A large deferred demand had been building up for goods
(especially durables) that were not available during the war. Moreover, although the sterling balances were, of course, a financial
liability, from the crude Keynesian view, they also represented
potential demand.

In the course of events, in 1946, the British economy was
aided by a 3-1/4-percent, $5. 0-billion loan, of which $3. 75 billion
came from the United States and $1. 25 billion from Canada. This
was supplemented by an additional $2. 7 billion in Marshall Plan
grants and loans from 1948 to 1951 (see Table 2. 5).

British policy appeared to be two-headed; the knowledge that
there was no lack of demand was accompanied by a contradictory,
but still persistent, fear of unemployment. Near the end of the war,
the editorial writer for the New Statesman thought that any attempt
to absorb German reparations would cause unemployment; and in
the same issue, we can find a report on Ernest Bevin's worries
about the potential redundant workers employed in the war industries,
who would be out of work in a civilian economy. [3] (Of course, economists in the United States were also worried about a postwar
depression.)

In the fall of 1945, I was in the Army Educational Program,
attending the University of Manchester. As did T. H. White, I somehow stumbled on a truth: "The one thing you will not have to worry
about," I told my fellow students, "is unemployment. You will be

TABLE 2.4

U. K. Money Supply As a Percent of National Income, Selected Years

Year	Net National Income (£ billion)	Quantity of Money* (£ billion)	Money as a Percent of National Income
1921	4.460	2.201	49.3
1926	3.914	1.990	50.8
1929	4.178	2.105	50.4
1934	3.881	2.209	57.0
1938	4.816	2.699	56.1
1945	8.480	5.825	68.7
1950	10.675	7.087	66.3
1955	15.325	7.931	51.8

*The quantity of money is the sum of the note circulation and clearing-bank deposits.

Source: F. W. Paish, Studies in an Inflationary Economy (New York: St. Martin's Press, 1966), p. 59.

TABLE 2.5

Marshall Plan Aid, April 3, 1948
to April 3, 1951

Recipient	Aid (thousands)
Britain	$2,703,049
France	2,223,880
Germany	1,188,757
Sweden	116,334
Belgium-Luxembourg	529,765
Netherlands	949,779

Source: Hadley Arkes, Bureaucracy, the Marshall Plan, and the National Interest (Princeton: Princeton University Press, 1972).

able to sell everything you make. You may have to work hard and
endure a reduced level of consumption, but business will be good
and the country will earn back its loans. At the end of just a few
years, you should be in much better shape than before the war and
enjoy very good incomes." (The venue for this discussion was a
pub in Manchester.)

The reaction to my remarks appeared to be that I was naive,
simple, and probably American. I was led to understand that I did
not comprehend the complexities of import-export relations (which
was true); nor did I understand how poor England was, now that she
was about to lose all her colonies.

I am not sure now that I was wrong. In 1978, I asked economists
what would have happened if England had removed the controls shortly
after the end of the war, and simply tried to sell all she could. The
problem of the sterling balances could have been solved by letting the
pound float, or by freezing the foreign-held balances into serial
bonds for eventual repayment. Of course, such a policy would have
elicited critical comments about British financial duplicity; the nasty
remarks would have possibly lasted for six months. (In 1978, in an
interview, Lord Robbins told me that the nasty remarks would have
lasted no more than "two weeks.")

The British fear was that opening the economy to the full force
of the market would destroy the credibility of the pound as a reserve
currency and would eventually cause the downfall of the City, i.e.,
the London financial industry—the complex of banks, investment
companies, and insurance companies that services and earns money
from a large international clientele. However, in retrospect, the
fear seems exaggerated; a more likely possibility is that the vast
demand for British goods, and shipping and services would have
surely set a reasonable floor to the value of the pound.

There is a question as to what would have been the effect on
the supply of real goods of opening up the economy. There was an
apparent fear that the flow of unrequited exports (goods sold for
sterling already held in foreign hands) would drain the British economy of its output, and that there would be no new net foreign funds
to buy raw materials for processing, or to import foodstuffs to feed
the population, and no domestic production left over to enjoy at home
or to use for capital formation. But this scenario was unrealistic in
terms of the workings of a competitive or business economy. In fact,
given good business prospects, the individual firms would surely
have been able to obtain credit or advances with which to buy raw
materials and pay wages, on the basis both of the productive potential
of their existing plants and labor force. (There was, at the end of
World War II, a shortage of all sorts of consumer manufactured
goods and especially of consumer durables.) A large part of these

credits, of course, would have been in foreign currency or convertible to foreign currency. The basic contention is that, given the strong market demand for their product, the true capital value of the British firms was quite high, and that they could have easily carried the debt required to finance the initial round of working capital. Wages would have settled at some decent level, because of the competition between firms to obtain and hold a work force. What was certain was that the business sector would have achieved a high rate of profit. This would have allowed for a quick repayment of the credits, or, as is more common in actual business, the retention of equity in the business sector's financial structure would have soon improved the debt/asset ratio. * Substantial profits would have elicited a high rate of real capital investment and a high rate of savings. The general results would have encouraged a spirit of enterprise and efficiency that would have allowed the British to keep pace with the continental competition and growth, once other economies, such as those of the French, Dutch, Belgians, Germans, and Italians, reentered the world export markets.

What, then, kept the British from following a free-market policy or something closely akin to it? There was, first, a continual underestimation of the strength of demand and the forces of growth. (Crosland, writing in the early 1950s, was pleasantly surprised by the growth of exports to 150 percent of the prewar level by 1949.)[4] Of course, this type of missed forecasting would not have seriously deterred a somewhat more market-oriented economy. In such a system, the individual agents would have automatically reacted to the pull of the economic environment by increasing output and capital investment. Missed forecasts may be considerably more harmful in a controlled economy where some authority is trying, more or less, to direct the allocation of resources.

There is a theoretical argument which illustrates this point. Suppose we have a centralized authority that is entrusted with making certain very important lumpy decisions (e. g. , the allocation of large units of capital investment). The central authority has the possibility of making precisely the right choice, in which case the exact optimum is reached. However, there is always a finite chance of error, in which case the total investment is misplaced and the waste or loss

---

*Aggregate business liabilities are usually not repaid in net terms; such items may be rolled over from one firm to another or through the banking system. However, in prosperous times, high profits and their retention increase the equity base, so that the debt-to-asset ratio becomes relatively small.

is considerable. Under the operations of a decentralized system, by contrast, the precise optimum can never be reached, since at random, some of the decision makers will place off target the resources they control. On the other hand, the modal point is probably correctly placed, and in any case, since some amount of the resources will be allocated properly, any loss is always partial. Which system is preferred involves the weighting of the probability of a potentially large loss against a certain recurring, but smaller, loss. Alternatively, we weigh the utility of expected larger returns combined with the possibility of a large loss, against the utility of a somewhat smaller but more assured return. (An analogy to this argument may be found in the theoretical justification for insurance, or in the role of effective diversification in portfolio theory.)

In the actual course of events, the British government appeared reluctant to set the economy free. Many of the wartime rationing controls were maintained until the advent of the Conservative government in the fall of 1951. Price controls on industrial goods persisted until 1951. Rationing of some goods was continued until 1954. Credit rationing was only abandoned in 1951.

In addition to an underestimation of growth, a major factor inhibiting the opening of the economy was a dislike of differential incomes. (Daniel Yergin notes that the attitude still persists; he reports on a conversation of Labor intellectuals vetoing the introduction of a new industry for fear that it would create British millionaires.)[5] If the economy had been freed up and a production upsurge ensured, then profits and the profitability of enterprise would have risen sharply. This factor would have pushed up investment and drawn out a high rate of saving;* and it would have been the motive force for increased efficiency, productivity, and refurbishing of capital equipment. However, the mode by which the results were achieved, if not the results themselves, would have been anathema to the socialists of the left, because profits are assumed to be the major sources of income inequality.

That in fact the government policies did succeed in reallocating income is evidenced by Table 2.6. Property income, which was 20 percent of the total British income in 1938, was down to 10 percent

---

*Consumption may or may not have fallen off under a more open policy. It is my contention that a working labor force attracts sustenance. In any case, Sir Stafford Cripps's austerity program kept imports to 86 percent of the prewar levels for the immediate postwar period. A market-determined system might have done as well through the encouragement of voluntary savings.

TABLE 2.6

Percentage Distribution of Postwar Personal Income
in the United Kingdom, 1938 and 1949

Item	1938	1949
Wages	37	47
Salaries	23	22
Armed-forces' pay	2	3
Mixed income	12	10
Property income	20	10
Social income	6	9
Total personal income	100	100*

*Original statistics do not add to 100.
Source: D. Seers, The Levelling of Incomes Since
1938 (Oxford: Oxford University, Institute of Statistics,
1951).

in 1949. Social income's proportionate share rose by 50 percent,
from 6 percent of total income, in 1938, to 9 percent of the total in
1949.

Looking at the evidence, the policies which directed and coddled
the economy, however, showed no great success in terms of encouraging growth. As can be seen from Table 2.7, the United Kingdom
lagged behind the rest of Europe in the rate of capital formation
during the postwar period. True, the rate was very close to that of
the United States, but other countries ran higher. And so England
did not narrow the income gap with the United States, as the rest of
Europe succeeded in doing (and as, of course, did Japan).

NATIONALIZATION AS A PREDETERMINED GOAL

At any rate, the realities of the postwar situation in no way
deterred the Labor party from implementing its predetermined program. Nationalization, in order to "capture the commanding heights
of the economy," was part of the agenda. Table 2.8 shows industries
nationalized or scheduled for nationalization during the years 1945-
51. Plans were also prepared for the nationalization of steel during
this time.

TABLE 2.7

Capital-Formation Ratios As a Percent of GNP, Selected Countries for Selected Years, 1945 to 1970

County	1945	1950	1955	1960	1965	1970	1975
Sweden	16.7%	19.8%	22.2%	22.0%	25.9%	22.0%	21.0%
United Kingdom	3.5	12.8	14.7	16.0	17.6	19.0	20.0
France	NA	19.6	18.5	20.0	25.6	23.0	23.0
Germany	NA	22.2	25.6	24.0	28.7	26.0	21.0
United States	4.9	17.0	18.0	18.0	18.0	17.0	16.0

Sources: Adapted from R. R. Mitchell, European Historical Statistics 1750–1970 (New York: Columbia University Press, 1975). Data for the United States are from the Department of Commerce.

TABLE 2. 8

Industries Nationalized, or Scheduled for Nationalization,
by Labor Government, 1945-51

Industry	Date of Nationalization
Bank of England	1945
British South American Airways	1946
BOAC—passenger	1946
British European Airways	1946
All coal mining, coke ovens, brickworks	1947
Railways, ships, docks, long-haul trucking	1948
All remaining electricity generation and distribution grid	1948
Gas distribution	1949
Steel (tentatively)	1951*

*Steel was denationalized by the Conservative government and
renationalized by Labor in 1967.

Source: Compiled by the author.

The industries slated for nationalization often appear to have
been selected more on the basis of ideological or historic reasons
than for any inherent economic rationale. In a mixed economy, the
obvious candidates for nationalization might be those industries which
can no longer operate on a workable competititve basis. (It is generally assumed that even free-enterprise societies may nationalize
those inductries which are natural monopolies, industries where
competition must necessarily entail a duplication of fixed facilities,
e. g. , electric-power distribution or perhaps rail connections between the same cities; an alternative is to operate these industries
as regulated utilities.) Nevertheless, Labor's prime candidate for
nationalization was the coal industry, not because it did not sell in
a competitive market, but perhaps because the coal miners had an
honored place in British labor history. It was thought that nationalization would reduce the level of labor disputes in the coal fields
because the coal miners would be more amenable to a management
derived from self-government. However, even in the short run,
nationalization did not forestall a debilitating coal strike in 1947 that
had a most unfortunate effect on overseas markets.

Moreover, because nationalization was pursued on a gentlemanly basis, it did not increase the "social wealth." That is, the firm's owners were given reasonably fair value for their holdings. (In those cases where there was no active market for the firm's securities, the owners were compensated on the basis of the present value of estimated net "maintainable revenues.")[6] It can be shown that when owners are truly compensated with the present value of the future flow of the earnings from their property, then "society" gains no wealth. Nationalization yields a true redistribution (or a net gain, if foreign owners are involved) only insofar as the existing owners are cheated or expropriated. * But the main drawback of British nationalization was that it diverted managerial energy and resources from other problems and endeavors, and it added an element of uncertainty to investment in other sectors of the economy that might eventually be subject to government takeover.

Roy Harrod argued that the postwar Labor government placed too much investment in the nationalized heavy industries, to the detriment of the lighter industries, which could have been refurbished with smaller absolute amounts. [7] However, Harrod's basic theme was that the government's investment program was excessive, given the voluntary level of savings at the existing full-employment level of national income. The effects of this excess of investment expenditures were suppressed inflation and balance-of-payment difficulties. The excess of aggregate demand was covered over by a system of rationing and controls that caused hardships by distorting output and inhibiting consumer choice. [8]

In making his analysis, Harrod is a strict Keynesian; he assumes a fixed level of savings and does not allow for the possibility that savings themselves might increase in a freer economy, which would allow the rate of return on savings (i.e., the interest rate or its equivalents) to rise. Nevertheless, the detailed Harrod arguments (if not the total model) are succinct and understandable. They are that commercial considerations—the comparison of the potential rate of return to the cost of capital—were ignored in allocating investments; and that, influenced by simpleminded sociologists' correlations between poor housing and such other social ills as crime or child abandonment, the government directed far too many resources into the construction and maintenance of subsidized housing.

---

*It is interesting to observe left-wing economists in the underdeveloped countries calling for the expropriation of foreign investments, while at the same time offering "fair" compensation. In fact, if fair compensation is to be given, the country would no doubt be better off using the funds to finance net new capital.

Of course, many of the nationalized industries were those which, in the United States, would be regulated, privately owned public utilities. In Europe, these industries generally tend to be publicly owned. There is an argument to the effect that if an industry is to be regulated, it might as well be nationalized, because in any case, it no longer operates under the efficiency constraints of competition. [9] Nevertheless, there is evidence that even in the case of the public utilities, nationalization tends to be more inefficient than regulation under private ownership. There are two important aspects in which a privately directed utility differs from a socialized industry. First, there is the considerable leeway that a rational utility commission may allow between the established rate of return and the realized rate. Essentially, the commission sets the utilities' prices to cover going costs and yield a normal return on capital. However, if the firm, by innovation or efficient management, manages to hold down costs and raise the return, a sensible commission will allow the company some time to enjoy this difference before calling for a reduction in the rates. Another aspect of the operation of the private utility is that the capital-investment and financing decisions are left to the company. This means that the rate of expansion and the capital intensity of the system are more or less determined by a rational discounting of future returns.* Under nationalization, the investment decision may be based on governmentally decided macrofiscal policies, so that the nationalized industry will be given more capital in a recession and less in a boom (or during a shortage of foreign exchange). If the nationalized industry is used in an investment balancing act for counter-cyclical policy, the resulting allocation of capital investment will not necessarily be optimal from the view of the microstructure of the economy.

Finally, a nationalized utility may tend to become overmanned. Overmanning simply means that the labor force (probably for political reasons) is larger than its optimum size. (Of course, this need not occur merely in the utilities; it is an obvious possibility in all nationalized industries where jobs may be given to political allies.) This does not happen as readily in a privately owned utility. The private

---

*There is an argument that government regulation of return (presumably, if the allowed rate of return exceeds the cost of capital) can lead to excess capital (overinvestment) in the regulated utility. I doubt if this argument really holds under conditions of growth; and I have not seen much empirical evidence supporting this thesis of Averch and Johnson. [10] (But, of course, in recent years the allowed return has probably been below the cost of capital.)

utility has an incentive for efficiency, since the company is only allowed the right to make a return. If the company does not keep its actual costs under control, it will not succeed in making the allowed return. * On the other hand, the government may encourage a nationalized industry to carry an extra-large labor force as a means of concealing the true level of unemployment during a downturn. It may become difficult to reshift this labor force to other industries during a subsequent recovery.

Of course, there are always many boards appointed and controls installed over socially owned utilities, and there are some positive and negative incentives to reduce waste. Whether these are as effective, in the long run, as the profit motive is questionable.

The capstone feature of the socialist program was the adoption of a comprehensive social security program—the Beveridge plan (security from the cradle to the grave) and the National Health Service. These plans were not necessarily completely mistaken. All modern countries may provide some income-support programs (Milton Friedman would advocate the negative income tax as the sole support measure for those below a minimum income level); and may provide some methods of assuaging social hardships, such as the costs of severe illness. The questions that arise are whether the British were well advised on the timing of these welfare programs, and the level or cost at which they were implemented. These programs could have been phased in more gradually, given the need for a high level of savings for the reconstruction and restructuring of the postwar economy.

The Beveridge program had another implicit flaw in terms of the postwar situation. The plan was not only directed toward providing income security, it was also designed to reduce unemployment essentially by decreasing the active labor force. This means it encouraged early retirement. † But in fact there was no lack of jobs in the postwar period; the problem was a lack of workers. A system which strength-

---

*It is possible to use a socialized industry to hold down prices in the short run, by selling at a price that does not cover a full return on capital. (Not that such a procedure may not be justified, say, in the case of off-peak pricing, or if, because of some historic mistake, the industry is overcapitalized.) However, when subsidized pricing is followed as a normal long-run procedure, some other sector of the economy must make up the loss.

†The U. S. social security system also has a bias toward early retirement. This bias begins to bite when the percentage of retirees grows relative to the work force. One cure is to reward later retirements.

ened attachment to the work force, by increasing the pension for de-
layed retirement, would have been more to the point.

The National Health Service, from the beginning, absorbed
more than its estimated budgeted costs. In 1949, a request was made
for an additional £52 million (a considerable sum for the period) to
cover the shortfall in the National Health Service budget. Of course,
part of the initial upsurge was due to a large demand for spectacles
and for dentistry in 1946 and 1947, and was no doubt partly explainable by past neglect; however, observers noted that the initial bulge
in costs did not tail off as the proponents of nationalized medicine
had argued it would. There developed a feeling that there was a tendency to overprescribe drugs, and a tendency to carelessly lose spectacles as long as replacements were completely free of charge.
Nevertheless, Aneurin Bevan resigned, as a matter of ideological
principle, in 1951 when the rest of the Labor cabinet voted to put a
nominal charge on false teeth and spectacles. It was estimated that
these charges would save £23 million yearly. *

Some of the effects of the Labor social programs show up in
Tables 2. 9 and 2. 10. In the immediate postwar period, the United
Kingdom was a high-consumption, moderate-growth country relative
to the rest of Europe. † A large part of the consumption can be
ascribed to the public sector. It might have been possible, under a
different set of policy formulations, to have increased the relative
share of investment (and savings) and reduced the share of private
and public consumption, with a resulting increase in the growth performance of the economy. It might even be true that this could have
been achieved without lowering the absolute level of consumption, if
an alternate set of policies could have improved incentives and increased the total output so that there could be more to invest, without
decreasing consumption. ‡

---

*The largest part, about 90 percent, of the financing of the
National Health Service comes not from the National Health Insurance
funds to which employees and employers contribute, but from general
funds.

†This was also true for the United States, but the United States
started from a higher base. Eventually the high-growth, high-capital-
formation countries of Western Europe caught up to the United Kingdom, passed it, and now have almost drawn equal with the United
States.

‡There are many references to the fact that American workers
got more output out of the same equipment than did the British. A
writer in The Economist ascribes some of the problem to the Marxist
inculcation in British labor, leading to a "they-versus-us" attitude. [11]

TABLE 2.9

Distribution of Gross National Product in the United Kingdom and Selected Countries, 1948 and 1951 (in percent)

Distribution of GNP	United Kingdom		France		Norway		Sweden		Netherlands	
	1948	1951	1948	1951	1948	1951	1948	1951	1948	1951
Private consumption	71.3	68.5	70.6	68.9	63.9	60.0	69.2	62.7	69.5	61.9
Public consumption	15.0	16.9	13.8	14.1	11.9	10.9	13.4	14.1	13.9	13.8
Gross domestic fixed investment	11.9	12.6	18.3	16.6	26.8	24.3	17.7	17.9	19.8	19.7
Change in inventories	1.0	3.9	1.9	1.5	3.7	3.8	1.3	2.7	4.0	5.0
Export surplus (+) or deficit (−)	0.8	−1.9	−4.6	−1.1	−6.3	1.0	−1.6	2.6	−7.2	−0.4
Gross national product	100.0	100.0	100.0	100.0	100.0	100.0	100.0	100.0	100.0	100.0

Source: Organization for European Economic Cooperation, Statistics of National Product and Expenditure (Paris: OEEC, 1938, 1947–55) OEEC, Paris, 1957.

TABLE 2.10

Annual Average Economic Growth Rates in the United Kingdom and Selected Other Countries, 1947–51 (in percent)

Country	Average Annual Economic Growth Rate, 1947–51	Ratio of Fixed Capital Investment to GNP in 1951	Ratio of Total Consumption to GNP in 1951
United Kingdom	3.4	12.6	85.3
Western European countries	4.4	14.6	81.2
France	9.5	16.7	82.9
Netherlands	5.8	19.7	75.7
Sweden	4.1	17.9	76.7
United States	5.2	16.3	79.4

Source: Organization for European Economic Cooperation, Statistics of National Product and Expenditure, 1938 and 1947 to 1955 (Paris: OEEC, 1957).

It can be argued that a lower level of effort and a relatively high level of consumption can result from a welfare economy. It may be that the provision of a large amount of free social services (a high level of transfer payments), especially when these are financed by direct progressive taxes on current earnings, can have a detrimental effect on incentives to earn additional income; and that such a system may, in addition, dampen the rate of savings by reducing their need. This argument does not appear in the standard macroeconomics texts because the classical Keynesians tended to consider only income effect and not the incentive effects of transfer payments. For example, the classical Keynesians thought that there would be no net income effects from a large, internally held national debt which was currently being serviced with taxes. Some people would have their incomes reduced by the taxes, and others would gain interest payments, but total aggregate income would be the same. However, as a counter-argument, consider the friction effects of the tax burden. The taxes fall on the currently producing part of the economy, causing all sorts of resource shifting, some falloff in incentives, and a reduction in economic efficiency. However, the interest payments are pure transfers; they do not reward any current output. The result of a high level of transfer payments could be a net fall in total output.

When the economic system is heavily weighted with social or welfare payments, the effects are likely to be even stronger. In this case, in his role of income earner or producer, the citizen runs up against increasing taxes as he earns or invests more; however, his share of social services, in money or in kind (such as free medical care or subsidized housing and food), does not depend on the amount of taxes he pays. These social services are provided free out of the general pot and in fact are likely to be more generous for lower-level taxpayers with lower incomes. One might achieve full employment in such an economy, but at a lower level of income and investment than might prevail under a system that provided fewer free social goods.

SUMMARY

The United Kingdom came out of the war in a better position than any of the other major European countries. In the period of 1945 to 1955, the British growth rate was not significantly different from that of the United States, and the growth of the economy was quite good in terms of Britain's own historic growth rates. However, a growth rate only equal to that of the United States widened the absolute gap between the two countries. Moreover, the growth rate actually achieved was disappointing in terms of the possibilities of the open markets awaiting manufactured goods. In the light of the evidence of what other European countries eventually accomplished, it should have been possible, under conditions of buoyant demand, for the U. K. economy to have narrowed the difference between the British and the U. S. output per capita.

At the end of the decade, the British economists, looking at the superior growth rate of the continent, presumed that this represented merely the catchup phase, and that when Germany and France equaled the British GNP per capita, their economies would taper off and, thereafter, merely grow at the same rate as England's. [12] (Such reasoning probably militated against joining the Common Market.)

In many ways, from the viewpoint of economic development, the immediate postwar decade was a lost opportunity. This period could have been used to establish British export markets quality and volume. The earnings generated could have been used to refurbish and revitalize the economy's capital base and to bolster its dynamic thrust. That the opportunity was not seized may be laid to several factors. There was the inordinate concentration of policy effort to fight a nonexistent specter of unemployment. There was a priority effort to equalize incomes, which resulted in a high level of direct taxes and heavy subsidies for housing and food. Policy was conditioned by a tendency to count up financial assets and show how they were outnumbered by financial liabilities. This led to the neglect of a proper assessment of the real conditions of the economic environment, which were really quite favorable. It might be noted that in a freer-market economy, such a wrong analysis would not have been as harmful. By definition, the real forces—that is, the potential profitability of existing capital and trained labor—would have asserted themselves naturally.

Among the factors slowing the potential rate of growth, we may count the diversion of effort involved in the politically motivated nationalization of various industries. Lastly, we have the probably premature direction of the economy toward a high consumption of public goods, to the detriment of savings and capital investment.

NOTES

1. C. A. R. Crossland, Britain's Economic Problem (London: Jonathan Cape, 1953), p. 11.
2. A. H. Hansen, Full Recovery or Stagnation (New York: W. W. Norton, 1938).
3. New Statesman and Nation, July 28, 1945, p. 50.
4. Crosland, op. cit., p. 41.
5. New Republic, August 4, 1978.
6. The Economist, December 1, 1945.

7. Roy Harrod, Are These Hardships Necessary? (London: Rupert-Hart Davis, 1947), pp. 76–77.

8. Many of the same arguments may be found in John Jewkes, Ordeal by Planning (London: Macmillan, 1948), pp. 234–36.

9. Henry C. Simons, Economic Policy for a Free Society (Chicago: University of Chicago Press, 1948), p. 5.

10. See Averch and Johnson, "Behavior of the Firm Under Regulatory Constraints," American Economic Review, December 1962.

11. The Economist, July 14, 1945, p. 34.

12. See J. Knapp and K. Lomax, "Britain's Growth Performance: The Enigma of the 1950s," in Economic Growth in Twentieth-Century Britain, ed. D. H. Aldcroft and P. Fearon (London: Macmillan, 1969).

3

GREAT BRITAIN TODAY: THE CONSEQUENCE OF BEING TOO GOOD

In the heyday of her prosperity, from the mid-1860s to the beginning of the twentieth century, the United Kingdom's per-capita growth rate was never over 1.9 percent per annum and generally averaged about 1.8 percent. [1] England's postwar real income growth of 2.2 percent per annum, per capita, from 1945 to 1975 was higher than in any other comparable stretch in her history, and therefore many authorities argued that this period could hardly be considered a failure, from the viewpoint of economic policy. However, success or failure is relative. England did not experience the economic exuberance of the rest of Western Europe. At the end of the 30-year period, England's absolute level of per-capita income was well below the levels of Sweden and the rest of her European rivals.

SOME DIAGNOSES AND REMEDIES

Up until the 1960s, the British could content themselves with the thought that the superior European growth record was mainly a matter of catchup, and that England still maintained a small absolute lead in per-capita income. This idea dissipated as the economic growth of the continent continued and Great Britain became the laggard. At this point, a mass of books poured forth that pointed out a variety of possible sources of England's economic debility and set forth a variety of possible cures. Details of these analyses are often very good, but sometimes the remedies seem simplistic. Thus, the authors of the Hudson Report recommend cutting the "American connection" and initiating French-style indicative planning. [2] One fails to see exactly how the American connection inhibited the British economy. Moreover, other countries have done quite well without indicative planning—that is, a set of bureaucratic central plans, which are never carried out 100 percent, anyway. (In the mid-1960s,indicative planning became a popularized concept among some development economists.)[3]

The diagnosis of Cambridge economists Godley and May is that the British economy is simply too "old" to successfully compete in the world markets;[4] a country whose industrial revolution started 160 years ago is too senile to engage in rough and tumble with newer economies. Further, an 80-year-old man does not run against 20-year-olds. After due thought this analogy does not hold. An economy is not old; people or machinery are old. There is no evidence that the British population is older than that of the rest of Europe; machinery can be replaced and organizations revamped. We have to look deeper to explain Britain's relative decline.

Apparently the Cambridge school's suggested cure for economic old age is to institute import quotas to solve the problem of foreign competition and the adverse balance of payments. Presumably, a few industries will remain sufficiently competitive to earn enough foreign exchange, to pay for food imports to feed the population. Full employment would be ensured by proper monetary and fiscal policy. The essential flaw in this solution is that it will lower real incomes. All sectors will have to accept the resulting drop in income. If any large militant segment of society refuses to accept its proportional cut in real income and opts, instead, to push its claim for a higher monetary income as an offset, the "little England" container will burst from the inward pressure.

A recent book by A. Glynn and Bob Sutcliffe ascribes the economy's bad tone to a fall in profitability. [5] (The book's description of the symptoms is quite good.) The rise in the wage share relative to other incomes has indeed eroded profitability (i. e. , profits and interest, divided by total assets). The fall in profitability has led firms to the increased use of debt financing. The resulting increase in risk eventually led to a precipitous decline in investment. The authors are Marxists who, following the Marxist scenario for the capitalist crisis, hold that the fall in profits is inevitable in a capitalist economy such as England. Their cure, of course, is a centralized dictated economy that will, no doubt, solve all problems. *

---

*It is a continual wonderment to me that the horrendous simplicity of the Marxist cure is so often missed. The basic Marxist program, as demonstrated in Eastern Europe, consists of force-feeding the rate of investment and forcibly restraining the growth rate of real wages and consumption.

SATISFACTION AND UNEASE

However, we must be fair. Before proceeding, we must note that although economists, businessmen, professionals, and technicians are not pleased with the performance of the British economy, the evidence of the public-opinion surveys indicates that a majority of Englishmen appear to be reasonably content with their lot. (See Tables 3.1-3.4.) In general, these polls seem to show that in general living contentment, the British rank below the Scandinavians and the Americans, somewhat below the smaller European countries, but above Germany, France, and Italy. On the other hand, the British see themselves as a poor nation, whereas the French and Germans consider themselves to be wealthy. Moreover, according to Table 3.4, the English are the most willing to emigrate, but then, for the British, there are many countries, such as Canada or Australia, where the culture shock of emigration would be minimal. Of course, measures of happiness are, by definition, subjective. The relative contentment of the English may be due to their infinite patience (moreover, they are convinced they live in a civilized country); the relative unhappiness of the French may be a result of their excitable and sensitized personalities. This is a great mystery.

Nevertheless, the dissatisfaction of the movers and doers of British society is quite real. Symptomatically, Robbins writes that it was humiliating in 1974 for the British to have to ask the Germans and French for funds to tide them over the international payment crisis. [6] (It means that the British consumption level was sustained, for at least a while, by the charity of its old enemies. Of course, at the moment, conditions have been lightened by the windfall flow of North Sea oil.) We have to ask what the long-run prognosis is for a society where dissatisfaction is heavily concentrated in the professional, technical, and managerial classes. [7]

It is this problem, essentially, that Samuel Brittan deals with in his book The Economic Consequences of Democracy. [8] Brittan's basic thesis is that a bare majority should not be considered sufficient for the formulation of economic policy. It is necessary to have rules of the game, to establish an implicit compact that existing rights, holdings, and capital may not be easily attacked or redistributed. If such a compact is not observed, a shifting coalition vote of 50+ percent may push the system into a cycle of despoliation. (It might be noted that the governmental system of the United Kingdom, where the executive comes out of the parliamentary majority, makes it comparatively easy to implement the views of the moment.) Where simple majority voting may easily change the rules of the economic game to favor those not pleased by the outcome, there is a reduced incentive to produce and to store physical or human capital.

TABLE 3.1

Comparative Levels of Satisfaction in Various Countries,
Major Items

Country	Your Life As a Whole	Your House- hold Income	Your Health
United States	.69	.41	.67
Denmark	.67	.54	.71
Ireland	.59	.32	.78
Netherlands	.57	.45	.66
Belgium	.51	.37	.63
United Kingdom	50	.37	.63
Germany	.41	.39	.48
France	.26	.17	.53
Italy	.17	.13	.43

Note: Rankings were made on a scale of 0 to 10.
Source: Survey of the Gallup International Research Institutes,
conducted for the Commission of the European Communities (Brussels
1979).

TABLE 3.2

Overall Satisfaction of the Swedes:
"How Do You Rate Your Country Overall
as a Place to Live In?"

Rating	1973	1975	1978
Very good	45%	68%	57%

Source: Swedish Psychological Defense
Research Institute, Stockholm, 1978.

TABLE 3.3

Perceptions Regarding Wealth of Own Nation:
"In Your Own Opinion, Do You Consider This a Wealthy Nation or a Poor Nation?"
(percentages of respondents)

Answer	United States Total	Canada Total	Western Europe							
			Total	United Kingdom	France	West Germany	Italy	EEC	Benelux	Scandinavia
Wealthy nation	89	91	47	19	77	89	9	52	80	76
Poor nation	4	1	24	46	3	2	56	24	2	5
Neither	5	6	25	32	18	—	32	20	17	18
Don't know/ no answer	2	2	4	3	2	9	3	4	1	1

Source: Gallup International Research Institutes, "Human Needs and Satisfactions, A Global Survey," conducted for the Charles F. Kettering Foundation, June 1977.

TABLE 3.4

Most Popular Nation for Emigration: "If You Were Free To Do So, Would You Like To Go and Settle, Permanently, in Another Country? If Yes, in Which Country?" (percentages of respondents)

Answer/Nation	United States Total	Canada Total	Western Europe Total	United Kingdom Total	France	West Germany	Italy	EEC	Benelux	Scandinavia
Desire to emigrate	8	9	14	22	17	8	17	16	15	11
United States	—	2	2	4	1	2	3	2	1	*
United Kingdom	*	*	1	*	*	1	1	1	—	*
France	*	*	1	1	—	*	1	1	3	1
West Germany	1	—	1	1	1	—	2	1	1	*
Italy	1	*	*	—	1	—	—	*	1	1
Switzerland	*	*	1	1	2	1	2	1	*	2
Spain	*	—	*	*	*	*	*	*	1	2
Australia	1	1	1	4	1	—	1	1	1	1
Canada	1	—	1	3	2	1	*	1	*	—
All other	2	2	3	7	7	*	3	4	4	1
Don't know/no answer	2	4	3	1	3	3	4	3	4	2
Don't desire to emigrate	89	86	80	71	81	84	81	79	74	85
Don't know/no answer	3	5	6	8	2	8	2	6	11	4

Source: Gallup International Research Institutes, "Human Needs and Satisfactions, A Global Survey," conducted for the Charles F. Kettering Foundation, June 1977.

SYMPTOMS AND CAUSES

It is difficult to point out which are the underlying causes and which are the symptoms of an economy's condition. The factors underlying the British problem are characteristically intermingled. The following factors have been pointed out as problem areas. (We may note that many of these same problems exist, to a lesser or greater degree, in other countries.)

1. union militancy; decline of work-force discipline; loss of worker morale;
2. the social and economic costs of absorbing a relatively large internal or external migration;
3. a misdirected educational effort; not enough educational effort spent on training managers and engineers;
4. the incentive-killing effect of high marginal tax rates;
5. slovenly or inefficient management;
6. poor productivity; overmanning in various industries;
7. the dampening of the entrepreneurial spirit;
8. the downward trend of company profits; the resulting increase in the debt-to-asset ratio (i. e. , increased leverage); the growing rate of financial failure, and the falloff in capital investment;
9. the burden of carrying too large a nonmarket sector.

As is apparent, the litany of complaints is long and complex. Let us discourse on a few of them.

Labor Morale and Productivity

The problem of labor morale and productivity has been endemic. The atmosphere is full of anecdotes about the bloody-mindedness of labor. For example, in the spring of 1978, the English papers contained a story of a worker at the Leyland plant who was fired for punching a foreman. Consequently, the worker's union threatened a walkout, and management reinstated the worker. At that point, the foremen and supervisors went on strike to protest the lack of protection from violent workers. [9] However, American condescension cannot last past the point of being reminded of the goings-on in the Chevrolet Vega plant in Lordsville, Ohio (1972), where disaffected young workers randomly sabotaged cars coming down the assembly line.

Nevertheless, the testimony of experts, as to the difficulties of labor management in the United Kingdom, piles up. The appropriate measure of the loss of labor efficiency from labor disputes is not just the man-hours spent on strikes; it should include the loss of human energy spent in harassment and diversionary tactics. * The many union shop stewards who are an integral part of the British industrial scene are always available to take on local complaints. This means that with a minimum of effort, disputes can be initiated on the floor and move up through the channels of managerial responsibility. It is reported that local labor disputes took up half the time of plant managers in the British car industry, compared with 5 to 10 percent quoted by plant managers in Belgium and West Germany. [11]

Although it is probable that realistic bargaining positions, in terms of the overall economy, are reasonably understood at the level of the union's central hierarchy and its staff, such positions can be abrogated at the lower levels of the organization. Observers have long noted the heavy proportions of shop stewards, and their disproportionate power, in the British labor structure. In 1971 there were 175,000 shop stewards, compared to 3,000 full-time union officers.[12] And to quote Lloyd Ulman, "The shop stewards are more likely to be involved with the vital details—the cutting edges—of collective bargaining than the officers of the national unions . . . and when, under pressure from a government with which they maintain close relations, national union leaders have attempted to restrain or supersede their stewards—as in the dock strikes of 1967—they have often been decisively rebuffed."[13]

In any case, the Trades Union Council (TUC) does not have much effective control over its constituent unions. This means that any general-guideline wage settlement is easily breached by the actions of the more militant unions, such as the miners or dock workers.

Along the same lines, Michael Shanks discusses the effect of further decentralizing labor power at the shop or factory level, in the context of overall planning. Such decentralization makes general policy more difficult to implement, because the local groups are more interested in the pay and the maintenance of the jobs at their particular plants than in the potential wage and the employment-generating capacity of the whole industry. [14]

There may be a cost attached to the proposed Sadlowski-type shop-floor democracy. Thus the continental unions are, on the whole, more centralized and ideologically oriented than the British unions.

---

*One writer half seriously suggests that the peculiar stubbornness of British labor relations may be a manifestation of a concealed, but longstanding, ethnic conflict between the Saxons and the Normans. [10]

TABLE 3.5

Unemployment in the United Kingdom, Selected Years

Year	Percentage of Labor Force Officially Unemployed	Year	Percentage of Labor Force Officially Unemployed
1900	2.5	1947	3.1
1905	5.0	1950	1.5
1910	4.7	1953	1.6
1915	1.1	1956	1.2
1920	2.4	1959	2.2
1923	11.3	1962	2.0
1926	12.7	1965	1.4
1929	11.0	1968	1.4
1932	22.5	1969	2.4
1935	16.4	1970	2.5
1938	13.3	1973	3.3
1941	2.2	1976	5.8
1944	0.5	1977	6.2

Sources: R. R. Mitchell, European Historical Statistics (New York: Columbia University Press, 1975); ILO Yearbook of Labor Statistics (Geneva: ILO, various issues).

However, many argue that their ideological commitment induces the European labor leadership to concentrate on problems of basic social change, leaving the management much more leeway to arrange the practical details of the everyday workplace.

Many ascribe the obdurate nature of British labor relations to the persistent fear of unemployment. Table 3.5 illustrates the long history of the unemployment problem in England. (It might be noted that British unemployment rates are understated, relative to the United States, since new entrants to the labor force currently seeking work are not included in the British count.) The British experienced significant unemployment in the 1920s, as well as the heavy unemployment resulting from the depression of the 1930s. The British fear of unemployment leads to make-work rules and to overmanning. Many economists had hoped that a sustained period of full employment (such as that prevailing in the post-World War II period) would reduce the fear of unemployment and thus ease labor resistance to

TABLE 3.6

Percentage of Labor Force Organized,
United Kingdom and United States, 1960

Labor Force	United Kingdom	United States
Entire labor force	43	26
Government workers	70	13

Source: L. Ulman, "Collective Bargaining and Industrial Efficiency," Britain's Economic Prospects (Washington, D.C.: Brookings Institution, 1968).

productivity-improving innovations. Unfortunately, this does not seem to have occurred. It is estimated that labor's demands, qualifications, and restrictions offset 75 to 80 percent of management-introduced innovations. [15] The reciprocal of overmanning is a low rate of productivity. British labor gets much less out of standard machinery, than does its American, Japanese, or European counterpart. (Andrew Gottschalk, of the London School of Business, told me that in the coal industry, the running time of modern machinery is only three hours out of each eight-hour shift.) And in spite of it all, the unemployment rate persists at around 6 percent.

One other point we might note (see Table 3.6) is the relatively early emergence of the public-employment unions in Great Britain. In 1960, 70 percent of the British governmental workers belonged to public-employee unions, compared to 13 percent in the United States. Labor unions in the public sector of the economy may be possibly more disruptive than the labor organizations in the market sector. In the market sector, there always exists the possibility that a costly wage settlement will raise the price of the product to a point which will bring about a noticeable fall in the quantity which can be sold and result in a subsequent drop in employment. Thus the market does exercise a tenuous, but nevertheless existing, restraint on the wage bargain. This restraint does not exist in the public sector, where the higher costs may be covered by compulsory taxes.

The British labor force is heavily unionized. There is a question as to how unions work. What is it that the union leadership seeks to maximize? If the union's goal is to maximize the total real wage bill in a given industry, they will consider the prospects for

growth in employment, in tandem with the level of wages, in formu-
lating their bargaining position. However, under the political pressures of the membership, the goal may become much shorter in
scope; it may only be to maximize the wage of those currently employed. Worse yet, the subconscious goal may be to maximize the
wage of those who remain employed; the leadership may not really
consider the problem of those who might be forced out of work after
the settlement. On a purely theoretical basis, a policy which reduced
employment could carry if a bare voting majority of the membership
remains employed. (Mancur Olson argues that the utility of the single
member, and the utility that he derives from the collective action of
the union, may not coincide. His argument stems from the problem
of "revealed preference" and the "free-rider" effect. Olson thus derives the compulsory need for maintaining union membership, presumably for the collective good of the group. [16] The Olson argument
can be stood on its head. What seems good wage settlement for the
older union members, who have seniority, is not always good for the
junior members who may find themselves unemployed or on part
time.) Of course, restrictive work rules and stipulations for maintenance of the work force may succeed, in the short term, in concealing the unemployment resulting from an extravagant wage settlement. Unfortunately, such make-work stipulations are most effectively
enforced in nationalized industries or in the public sector.

Recruiting Managers

About equal to the volume of complaints about low productivity
in the use of labor are the complaints about the difficulties of recruiting and rewarding engineers and professional management. The
explanations for this problem may be classified as either sociological
or economic.

Among the explanations offered for the lack of management
talent and of aggressiveness is the British historical tendency to
recruit young brains for government, literature, the ministry, the
universities, or the colonies, and the tendency to downplay engineering and business. [17] Presumably, the Victorian ethos left the practical running of affairs to gifted amateurs (a develishly attractive
idea), but a device that is hardly adequate in the present technically
minded world. It is true, of course, that British engineering had
some superb accomplishments in the nineteenth century, but this is
ascribed to the work of practical men with shop experience. Industrial
research and development in the latter half of the twentieth century
requires the staff work of highly trained scientific engineers and
administrators. It is difficult to acquire any hard evidence for this

TABLE 3.7

Emoluments of Senior Employees, Imperial Chemicals
(in pounds)

Emoluments (Salaries)	Tax	Take-Home Pay	Number of Employees	
			1975	1976
10,001-12,500	5,300	7,200	745	1,052
12,501-15,000	7,000	8,000	285	434
15,001-17,500	8,800	8,700	173	187
17,501-20,000	10,700	9,300	58	135
20,001-22,500	12,700	9,800	52	47
25,501-25,000	14,700	10,300	21	40
25,001-27,500	16,800	10,700	9	18
27,501-30,000	18,900	11,100	13	12
30-001-32,500	21,000	11,500	6	11
32,501-35,000	23,000	12,000	4	8
35,001-37,500	25,100	12,400	8	5
37,501-40,000	27,200	12,800	1	2
40,001-42,500	29,300	13,200	1	4
42,501-45,000	31,300	13,700	1	1
45,001-47,500	33,400	14,100	—	1

Source: Imperial Chemicals, Annual Report (London, 1976).

line of argument, except that the outlays of the British educational system for the training of engineers and scientists seem disproportionately low. Of course, the British made many bright discoveries in radar, aeronautics, nuclear energy, and television in the twentieth century. The problem may not lie in the supply of highly trained engineers or administrators, but in a shortage of adept personnel, able to implement innovation, who are turned out in quantity by the standard American universities and colleges.

Another strand of argument goes that it is not very psychologically rewarding to be an engineer or a manager in England, since a large part of one's time will be spent hassling with the shop steward.

Although there seems to be an element of truth in the sociological arguments, the economic factors would seem to be the overriding ones. Presumably brains, talents, and push would enter the engineering and managerial ranks if the economic rewards compensated for the difficulties. (Moreover, a mass infusion of talent into the management ranks would have broken through some of the institutional barriers that have slowed down the efficient organization of the firm.) But in actual fact, in postwar Britain the opposite development took place. As the difficulties of management grew, the relative real after-tax salaries declined.

Table 3.7 illustrates the practical impact of high marginal tax brackets on the managerial employees of an actual company, Imperial Chemicals, Ltd. It can be noted that for what one might consider a moderately good income, £21,250 per annum (about $41,000), the take-home pay is £9,800 (about $19,000); a salary raise of £2,500 ($4,800) yields only about a £500 ($900) increase in after-tax income. The combination of high taxes at the margin and low psychic rewards no doubt explains the complaints about the shortage of good subordinate staff—the noncoms and the lieutenants of industry who carry the esprit de corps of the organization.

The high taxes lead to a multiplication of managerial perquisites (commonly known as perks). These are forms of consumption, such as company cars and business travel, that are passed through by the corporation and thus escape taxation. The old English virtue of straightforwardness is eroded. It is common to make do on the fiddle, i.e., enjoy the use of nontaxable real income. Of course, all this diverts effort which might otherwise be expanded on more productive endeavors. Moreover, since the mix of goods and services obtained through the perks might not be the same as that which would be chosen out of the equivalent money income, consumer utility is not maximized.

Profits, Real Wages, and Employment

As is also true in the United States and Sweden, Britain has experienced a decline in the profitability of the private corporate sector, when profitability is measured as a rate of earnings over assets invested. Such a decline in profitability may be concealed for a while by the firm's assuming increased financial risk; that is, by increasing the use of debt, relative to ownership capital, in the financial structure of the company. This phenomenon is apparent in Sweden, the United States, and Britain; the debt-to-asset ratio has been growing at a significant rate in all three countries. (In the United States, the use of debt financing is called leverage; in England, gearing. In Sweden, the phenomenon is measured inversely by the equity-to-asset ratio, called solidity.)

The use of debt will enhance or help maintain the nominal rate of return on equity capital, even if the rate of return on the total assets invested in the firm is declining. The use of debt financing is particularly attractive in an inflationary environment. However, the apparent advantage of debt financing begins to erode as the nominal interest rate rises to compensate for the rate of price-level rise and to cover the enhanced lender's risk. A high debt structure hardly speaks for the vitality of the private sector. It means that in case of a downturn, the lender of last resort is likely to be the public treasury. We might note that the resulting government loans that are given in the most extreme financial difficulties are seldom a one-shot deal; they may evolve into a continuing arrangement of subsidies, or eventually the government inherits a loss-making industry. The latter might be called achieving nationalization by default.

In the theoretical model of the static economy, a decline in profitability may be the endogenous result of a deepening supply of capital, which lowers the marginal productivity of capital. (In classical economics, this simply means that as the supply of capital becomes more abundant, relative to the other factors of production, its price will fall.) However, in the actual working of a real world system, the return on capital can be reduced by exogenous factors, such as an arbitrarily high level of labor costs or a biased tax system. * A low rate of return on capital reduces the level of savings-investment (i.e., the rate of capital formation) and growth.

---

*Marxist economists may see, in the decline of profits, an illustration of the inherent contradiction of the capitalist system. Of course, they seem not to take notice that the forced growth of the Communist economies is fueled by compressing the real wage of the workers.

In the classic Keynesian situation, when there is a shortfall of expenditure on real capital investment, the economy experiences falling prices, an increase in unemployed labor, and low profits. The prescribed cure is an expansion of aggregate demand, which increases both employment and profits. The price level, as Keynes tells it, will inch up slightly, money wages will be relatively stable, and real wages decline minimally; but total real wages will increase. * However, the current situation facing the major industrial countries is somewhat different from the classic Keynesian case. Although there is considerable unemployment, both prices and money wages appear to react upward to every increase in aggregate demand; on the other hand, there is a general consensus that the return on real assets is relatively low. In this situation, one might begin begin to pose the neoclassical economic questions hesitantly broached by the symposium of British economists in the <u>Midland Bank Review</u> of February 1977.[18]

The questions posed are: "What proportion of unemployment is actually due to too high real wages? And does any reduction in unemployment necessarily involve a reduction in real wages?"

The authors' answers to these questions are essentially negative (although it is a sign of the times that the questions should be raised at all). However, their analysis seems to be set in a static framework; that is, as if one could cut wages and then see if unemployment would increase. The question might be put this way. Suppose there were a competitive wage system so that the nominal wage would not increase as long as there were significant unemployment. Now, suppose we have a steady-as-you-go fiscal-monetary policy to stabilize aggregate demand. Prices might rise somewhat, total output and employment would rise, and profits and investment would rise; the real wage unit would have fallen, but the total of the real wages, which comprises the number employed, times their wage, would have risen because of the rise in the number employed. (Nevertheless, the real wage unit of the already employed would have dropped.)†

---

*This increase in the real wage total results because even if the real wage unit declines slightly, employment increases more than proportionately. This is likely to be true even for the individual worker, since he may now be offered a full workweek. It seems clear that although Keynes had no use for downward flexibility in the money wage, he hoped that the real wage unit would show some downside flexibility during the recovery period.

†The analysis has been cast in Keynesian terms for the sake of simplicity. The real balance, or Pigou-effect analysis, is not the appropriate analytical model here because the assumed situation is

If the results of this scenario seem plausible, it follows that the pre-existing real wage must have been too high.

There are two thoughts one might like to interpose at this point. There is a further paradox that although such a successful full-employment policy might reduce the gross real wage of some particular workers, it still might increase their real after-tax wage. This results because a large part of the transfer payments supporting the unemployed are financed by wage and salary taxes. Thus even in this case, the sacrifice for almost all individual workers might be nil. The second thought is that it is difficult to conceive how one would engineer a cut in the level of the real wage unit in the present political-economic climate in the United States or the United Kingdom.

THE ELTIS-BACON THESIS

So all the items in the litany of complaints are more or less true. The problem is to find some thread of interrelatedness: Is there any common theme which binds the elements together?

While it does not answer all questions, such a theme is broached by two young economists, Robert A. Bacon and Walter Eltis, who argue that the basic problem is the excess production of social goods. This involves a deleterious diversion of output from the productive or market sector of the economy to the nonmarket sector. The result is a distortion of choice, a lowering of growth, and a fight over income shares. [19]

Let us explain further. There is an old expression which goes, "Too good is no good." In one sense, it may mean that in the affairs of this world, an attempt to be uncritically kind, and to give to and share with all may be self-defeating. It may be that the provider of goodness will exhaust his resources without really improving the lot or happiness or self-esteem of the recipients. In a modern economy, a large part of the role of being good is left to the government and its agencies. The government does good by providing the public with social and health services; subsidizing such items as basic housing or food, and education; and transferring money income to the poor. Clearly, these services are mostly meritorious (or at least they fit somebody's notion of merit), but just as clearly, the government's

---

not one of parallel falling prices and wages. The starting point is a situation where a level of rigid money wages has been reached, which has raised the natural rate of unemployment and reduced the rate of return on capital.

services are not free. They are financed by taxing away resources that might otherwise go to other sectors of the economy.

It is obvious that a large amount of merit goods would still be provided even without the intervention of the government. They would be financed by private charity or by group insurance. Of course, the amount and distribution of the merit goods might be different from that provided by governmental policy.

Most economists (except for the radical or libertarian anarchists) are agreed on a role for the public sector. The government should provide goods or services where there is a large degree of commonality; where there is a divergence of marginal private utility from marginal social utility, or a divergence of marginal private cost from marginal social cost; where the individual utilitities (or disutilities) are interrelated; where there are strong neighborhood effects; or where there are external economies or diseconomies not reflected in the pricing system. These criteria are all interrelated. They mean that there are certain activities which, left purely to the market system, would not be provided at a socially desired quantity (or activities such as the level of pollution control, which might be fostered at a quantity above a social and economically acceptable minimum). To furnish a homely example, as a citizen, I derive a benefit from having all the children in my area educated (at least up to a certain level), whether or not I am a child or even a parent of one or more children currently being educated. Since the benefits of education may extend beyond those to the particular child or family, and since the community does not wish to see any children deprived of education because the price may appear too high to their family, the community decides to finance education out of a general tax and furnish it as a free public good. The problem with public goods is always how far and how much.

Bacon and Eltis place most of the blame, in the failure of the British economy to keep up with its neighbors, on the excessive growth of the nonmarket or nonprice sector, relative to the rest of the economy. The nonmarket sector includes a large part of the government's activity. It includes the employment and output of all goods and services that are provided free, such as health, education, or police protection; the amounts by which certain goods are subsidized, such as council (i.e., public) housing; and expenditures made to cover the deficits of nationalized industries, such as the $1 billion spent to cover the out-of-pocket losses of British Steel in 1977. It does not include the output of the nationalized industries where these goods are sold at a price sufficient to cover costs. The advantage of this definition is that it makes it possible to make comparisons between countries having different levels of nationalized industries.

The economic impact of the nonmarket sector may be considered from two aspects. The first is from the view of the demand for personal income. The goods and services of the nonprice sector are provided free to the individual. Working harder will not enable one to purchase more or to obtain goods and services of a better quality. As a matter of fact, an increase in earnings may reduce one's legal right to grants or subsidies, propel one out of some of the share in the nonprice or subsidized sector, and force one to purchase the equivalent service in the market sector; in such a case, one may end up with a reduction of real income.

The second aspect of the existence of a nonmarket sector is that it must be financed. This means that when the nonmarket sector is relatively large, the tax rate must rise. If the tax system has a high proportion of direct progressive taxes levied on profits and personal incomes, the net return for increased effort, investment, or efficiency may be very low. Considering that after a point, there is a rising psychological cost (rising marginal disutility) of increased effort, the effect of high marginal taxation must dampen incentives. Thus we have the two sided effects on economic incentives of a high-tax, large free-public-goods-sector economy. Free goods dampen the need for additional income; high progressive taxes reduce the reward for additional effort and investment in capital.

We might also, at this point, consider the effects of direct progressive taxes versus indirect or consumption taxes. Indirect taxes, excises placed on the sale or use of goods and services, also lower net real income. However, since these taxes tend to be proportional or regressive in operation (that is, for these taxes, the proportion of tax to income does not rise with additional income and may even fall), incentives are not as blunted as they are under high progressive taxes. On the other hand, regressive taxes (essentially those placed on standard consumption items), by definition fall most heavily on the lower-income groups.

And in fact, there is evidence to the effect that the after-tax income in the United Kingdom is on the egalitarian side of the scale. Table 3. 8 is excerpted from a study by Peter J. Wiles, and provides his estimate of the after-tax income distribution for various countries. (We will not go into all the difficult data problems cited in the original table.) What Wiles presents is a relative scale giving the proportionate income of each income group in comparison to the mean. Thus in the United Kingdom in 1969, the upper fifth percentile of the income recipients received incomes approximately 2. 5 times the mean income; the upper tenth percentile about 2 times the mean. In the United States, for 1974, the upper fifth percentile received 2. 9 times the mean income; the upper tenth percentile, about 2. 3 times the mean income. As can be seen in the table, the Swedish

TABLE 3.8

After-Tax Income Distribution for Various Countries

Percent of Income Versus		United Kingdom		Italy	Hungary		Sweden		Canada	United States	
Median Income		1953-54	1969	1969	1967	1972	1967	1971	1971	1950	1974
P_{95}/P_{50}	%	251.1	251.4	331.0	201.0	206.5	231.1	226.0	300.0	315.6	289.8
P_{90}/P_{50}	%	194.5	204.4	234.0	171.5	173.3	197.0	182.5	226.7	200.0	229.4
P_{75}/P_{50}	%	143.2	149.2	154.7	134.2	140.8	148.4	138.1	153.7	160.0	153.0
P_{25}/P_{50}	%	73.3	71.2	61.5	75.3	76.7	71.7	74.5	64.8	58.0	63.5
P_{10}/P_{50}	%	52.9	52.0	39.9	57.3	57.0	53.7	51.0	38.4	28.1	30.7
P_{5}/P_{50}	%	43.5	42.5	29.5	50.0	48.4	35.8	25.3	25.0	15.7	23.9

Source: Peter Wiles, in Income Distribution, ed. Krelle and Shorrocks (London: Institute of Economic Affairs, 1978).

55

TABLE 3.9

Nonmarket Purchases of Marketed
Output as a Proportion of
Marketable Output

Year	Excluding Defense	Including Defense
1955	23.5%	31.5%
1960	24.2	31.0
1965	24.9	30.5
1974	31.4	35.9
1975	32.4	36.9

Source: Excerpted from Robert
Bacon and Walter Eltis, Britain's Economic Problem: Too Few Producers,
2d ed. (London: Macmillan, 1976).

and British income distributions are considerably more equal than
those of the United States or Canada. Sweden has a somewhat more
even distribution than the United Kingdom in the upper groups, but
the very lowest fifth percentile did considerably better in the United
Kingdom than in Sweden. (In these kinds of analysis, one should
always take the lowest percentiles with some caution; they may, for
example, include retired people living on their capital.)

In any case, going back to Eltis's and Bacon's main point,
illustrated in Tables 3.9 and 3.10, over the period 1960-75, the
largest portion of British growth went to the common-goods, nonprice sector. The portion of the nonmarket sector's purchase, of
market-sector output, as defined by Bacon and Eltis, went up from
24.2 percent in 1960 to 32.4 percent in 1975. (Alternatively, the
government's gross share of the GDP went from 36 percent to 45
percent in the same period.) One interesting statistic (in Table 3.10)
shows that from 1968 to 1975, the annual rate of growth of market-
sector output that was reinvested or consumed in the private sector
was only 0.4 percent. This has dampened growth because it indicates
a diversion of resources from the private sector, and the reduction
in the funds that could be invested, in productive real capital, in all
sectors of the market economy. It might be noted that Eltis and Bacon

TABLE 3.10

Growth Rates in Market Output, and in Market and Nonmarket
Consumption and Investment

Item of Growth	1955-65	1965-75	1955-75
Annual growth rate in real market- sector output	3.6%	1.3%	2.5%
Annual growth rate in real market output remaining in market sector	3.7	0.4	2.0

Annual growth rate in real marketable
    output invested and consumed by
    nonmarket sector
	3.4	3.3	3.4

Annual growth in real market output
    consumed by privately generated
    income
	2.9	0.6	1.8

Source: Excerpted from Robert Bacon and Walter Eltis, Britain's Economic Problem: Too Few Producers, 2d ed. (London: Macmillan, 1976).

(as Harrod did earlier) reject the fallacy which insists on placing the bulk of investment in heavy industries. This fallacy seems to be recurrent in socialist thinking; it assumes that somehow true growth derives only from the development of heavy industry.

The annual growth in real private consumption out of market-generated incomes, from 1965 to 1975, has been only 0.6 percent. The productive workers, those working in trade, commerce, finance, transportation, power, mining, agriculture, and manufacturing, have transferred resources at an increasing rate to the nonmarket (nonprice) sector of the economy. At the heart of the matter is the effect of an inordinately large nonmarket sector on the intensity of the struggle for income shares. Although the nonmarket sector's goods and services go back to the citizens, it may not provide the goods in the amounts and the mix that would be demanded under conditions of free choice. Bacon and Eltis lay the militancy of British labor mainly on this factor.

The growth in the public sector could be accommodated if a strong central trade-union leadership persuaded the rank and file to exercise wage restraint, to allow for the increase in social goods.

"But . . . workers will not necessarily acquiesce in a reduction in the rate of increase of private consumption per head from 2.8 percent to 0.9 percent for thirteen years."[20]

The same problem holds where the government expands the level of transfer payments. As Josselyn Hennessy writes, "It is only too easy to pass an act creating additional credits for health or pensions, and there is no objection to this providing that political, industrial and trade union leaders take care to ram it home to the people that they will not get these benefits free."[21]

One result of the growth of the nonmarket sector, then, is that the labor force becomes frustrated at the fall in the growth of the real wage, stemming from the outcome of policies which have never been clearly explained. Such frustrations set off a spate of explosive wage demands. Of course, the monetarist economists may argue that the increased wages from settlements would not result in price inflation if there were a steadfast, restrained monetary policy. However, once the new wage bargain is made, price stability can only be achieved by accepting an increase in unemployment.* Moreover, the increase in unemployment entails a fall in capacity utilization, which means a fall in profits. Apparently, in recent British policy (as is true in the United States), there has been a compromise between the two evils. There has been an increase in price levels and an increase in unemployment. Depending on one's economic persuasion, one might say that the upward push in the nominal wage has worsened the tradeoff between inflation and unemployment (has shifted the Phillips curve to the right), or that it has increased the natural rate of unemployment. (The outcome in either case is the same.)

MONETARY POLICY

A rough picture of British monetary policy can be obtained from Tables 3.11 and 3.12. Considering the transaction demand behavior of cash and demand deposits, we may note that the rising growth rate in the M_1 money stock in the 1970s also brought about a concurrent increase in velocity. (The inverse of velocity is the amount of money stock held relative to the measure of economic activity.) This rise in velocity may be ascribed to the effect of

---

*What the monetarists would need, to make their policies work, is a set of labor leaders who are quick learners. They would need to grasp the fact that untoward wage demands that were not ratified by the monetary authorities would lead to unemployment.

TABLE 3.11

United Kingdom: M_1 Money Growth, Price-Level Changes, and Employment, Selected Years, 1946-77

Year	M_1 (in millions of pounds sterling)*	Annual Rate of Growth of M_1	Income Velocity of Money Supply (GDP/M_1)	Annual Rate of Change, Consumer Price	Official Rate of Unemployment
1946	4,960	—	2.6X	—	—
1949	5,190	1.5%	2.7	5.8%	2.0%
1953	5,853	3.1	2.8	5.9	1.5
1955	6,010	1.3	3.2	2.5	1.4
1958	6,094	0.4	3.7	3.5	1.3
1961	6,761	3.5	4.0	1.5	1.9
1964	7,557	3.8	4.4	3.1	2.0
1967	8,443	3.8	4.7	3.7	1.9
1970	9,635	4.5	5.3	5.5	2.5
1973	13,303	11.3	5.4	8.6	3.3
1974	14,739	10.8	5.6	15.9	2.6
1975	17,481	18.6	5.9	24.2	4.1
1976	19,467	11.4	6.3	16.6	5.8
1977	23,660	21.5	5.9	15.8	6.2

*M_1 = currency in circulation, plus demand deposits.

Sources: International Monetary Fund, International Financial Statistics (Washington, D.C.: IMF, 1946-77); International Labor Organization, Yearbook of Labor Statistics (Geneva: ILO, 1949, 1951, 1959, 1968, 1977).

TABLE 3.12

United Kingdom: Growth in Money Stock—M_2, Selected Years 1946-77

Year	M_2 (in millions of pounds sterling)*	Annual Rate of Growth of M_2	Income Velocity of M_2 (GDP/M_2)
1946	6,820	—	1.9X
1949	7,230	2.0%	2.0
1953	8,755	4.9	1.9
1955	8,838	0.5	2.2
1958	9,593	2.8	2.4
1961	10,705	3.7	2.5
1964	12,025	4.0	2.8
1967	14,840	7.3	2.7
1970	17,947	6.5	2.8
1973	33,141	22.2	2.2
1974	37,430	12.9	2.2
1975	40,100	7.1	2.6
1976	44,638	11.3	2.7
1977	48,773	9.3	2.9

*M_2 = currency in circulation, demand deposits, plus savings deposits.

Source: International Monetary Fund, International Financial Statistics (Washington, D.C.: IMF, 1946-77).

anticipated price-level rises, which cause users of demand deposits to economize on their transaction cash balances. (Expected rises in the price level increase the nominal interest rate; this in effect raises the explicit or imputed costs of holding noninterest-bearing transaction cash, and leads to a reduction in cash balances relative to the level of transactions.) However, whereas the velocity of the M_1 money stock shows a perceptible rise in the 1970s compared to previous periods, the demand for money, according to Milton Friedman's preferred broader definition, M_2 (i.e., currency, demand deposits, and interest-bearing time deposits at the banks) was quite stable (see Table 3.12). This means that the rate of change in M_2 and the rate of change in nominal (money) income ran a parallel course.

However, more to the point of our present argument, we may observe the rising rate of unemployment from 1970 on. Whether measured in terms of M_1 or M_2, there has been a rapid acceleration in the rate of increase in the money stock. Sadly, however, this increase has done little to reduce the 6 percent level of unemployment. The money-supply increase has vented itself almost wholly in driving up the level of inflation to 16 percent; and so much for the policy belief regarding the Phillips-curve tradeoff, that a higher level of inflation would at least reduce the level of unemployment. The data seem to add supporting evidence to Friedman's argument that the level of unemployment may, at a certain point, be determined by the structure and relative flexibility of the labor market (i. e. , the natural rate of unemployment). If the actors in the economy anticipate the rate of change in the money stock and the resultant rate of price-level increases, expansive monetary policies will have no effect on the level of employment.

We might also interject at this point that the monetary experience of Sweden shows similar results. Moreover, oddly enough, the velocity of the money stock in the two countries, measured in terms of M_2, is almost identical.

Fall in Profitability and Debt Financing

In recent years, the labor powers in the United Kingdom have made at least part of the push in nominal wages stick. According to Eltis and Bacon, the increase in real take-home pay from 1963 to 1973 averaged 2. 2 percent per annum. (It actually decreased from 1973 to 1975.) However, real take-home wage growth would have only averaged 0. 9 percent per annum from 1961 to 1974 if the workers had made their proportionate contribution to the increased cost of the nonmarket sector. The discrepancy in these two trends has come out of the profit share of national income.

As we have noted previously, the fall in profitability has encouraged the use of debt financing. Table 3. 13 shows the change in the average financial structure of British operating companies from 1953 to 1976. The debt level has risen from 32 percent to 51 percent of total financing. As has been discussed earlier, it does appear that the managerial cure for a fall in real profitability is to increase the degree of leverage (the proportion of debt) in the financial structure. Since the explicit interest rate on debt is always less than the desired rate of return on ownership equity (Adam Smith offhandedly observed that the ratio between the commercial interest rate and the desired return on the owner's stock would be about two times), and

TABLE 3.13

Comparison of the Financial Structure of British
Industrial and Commercial Companies,
1953, 1961, 1972 and 1976

Financial Item	1953	1961	1972	1976
Current liabilities	25.6%	26.3%	31.4%	39.9%
Long-term debt	6.5	8.0	19.6	10.7
Total debt	32.1	34.3	51.0	50.6
Deferred tax	N.A.	3.2	3.6	7.9
Preferred shares	8.9	5.1	0.6	0.6
Common equity	56.1	55.2	40.6	38.5
Minority interest	2.9	2.3	4.2	2.4
Total equity	67.9	60.6	45.4	41.5
Total liabilities and capital	100.0	100.1	100.0	100.0

Sources: 1953 data adapted from Brian Tew and R. F.
Henderson, eds., Studies in Company Finance (Cambridge,
England: National Institute of Economic and Social Research,
1959), statistical appendix, table A02, p. 270; 1961, 1972,
and 1976 data adapted from Central Statistical Office, U.K.
Financial Statistics (London).

since interest is deductible before the payment of the corporate-
profits tax, the increase in the proportionate use of debt financing
may shelter the apparent or accounting rate of return on equity, at
least for a while. (This procedure is apparently running its course
in the United States and Sweden, as well as in Great Britain.) However, the short-term financial cure of increasing debt has harmful
side effects. The financial markets are not fooled for long. The
borrower's risk and the lender's risk rises; interest rates rise and
the rate of return required by the market for investment in shares
also rises; the overall cost of the mix of capital funds rises. Risk
taking in new investment is inhibited. [22] (Defensive investment in
standard enterprises is encouraged over investment in innovative,
creative, and risky fields.) The increase in the bankruptcy carries
with it the potential for disruption in the operations of financial
institutions and in the financial markets.

It may be argued that bankruptcy does not involve any additional costs over the economic losses already sustained by the original misdirection of investment. The underlying cause of any financial failure is the initial bad forecast of the returns from the project. It is true that an informal creditor composition or a formal bankruptcy reorganization merely involves the reshuffling of claims from equity holders to creditors, in acknowledgement of the writedown of the economic value of the initial investment. However, even if this were approximately true, bankruptcy reorganization would result in either nationalization or a private-creditor takeover and, very likely, the dismissal of the present management. This, too, would be an inhibiting factor in the rate of capital formation.

Internal Migration

Some of the details of the total Eltis and Bacon scenario may not be exact. The argument does not explain all the trouble areas in the British economic structure. Nevertheless, the shift of resources from the price sector (whether private or nationalized industry) to the public nonmarket sector does represent a real transfer burden that may have been prematurely fastened onto the British economy. Something of an analogy is provided by the economy of the city of New York, where in the period 1960 to 1976, nonmarket-sector employment fell from 3.13 million to 2.64 million, a decline of 15 percent. In the same period, nonmarket employment peaked in 1974, at 581,000, before the fiscal crisis caused a cutback. The fiscal overburden resulting from carrying more governmental services on a declining tax-paying base caused an exodus of human and physical capital from New York City. This further weakened the tax base, necessitating additional increases in tax rates, and triggering a disastrous downward cycle.

In the more centralized fiscal system of Great Britain, taxes do not vary significantly by locality. Therefore, the phenomenon of fiscally induced local migration is not as likely. However, an overburden of taxes could produce an introverted migration; that is, there could be an exodus of effort from the market economy to private pursuits—more time and devotion would be spent on the garden, and less on the shop floor.

Presumably, there is nothing wrong with lazing it through, if that's what people truly want. There may be something wrong with a system which biases the choice.

The intent of this study is to compare developments in two socialistic economies, Sweden and Great Britain. This chapter and the previous one highlighted the anomalies and contradictions that have constricted the postwar British economy. The next chapter consists of a sketch of the Swedish economy with contrasts to the British economic structure whenever these seem to furnish a useful explanation of the different course of development in the two countries.

NOTES

1. See Phyllis Deane and W. A. Cole, British Economic Growth—1688-1959 (Cambridge: Cambridge University Press, 1962).

2. The United Kingdom in 1980: The Hudson Report (New York: Wiley, 1974).

3. See J. Hennessy, V. Lutz, and G. Scimone, Economic Miracles (London: Institute of Economic Affairs, 1964), for a skeptical view of the actual efficacy of such planning.

4. See Wynne Godley and Robert M. May, Economic Policy Review (Cambridge: Cambridge University Press, 1978).

5. A. Glynn and Bob Sutcliffe, Capitalism in Crisis (New York: Pantheon, 1972).

6. Lionel Robbins, Aspects of Post-War Economic Policy (London: Institute of Economic Affairs, 1974).

7. Patrick Hutber, The Decline and Fall of the Middle Class (Harmondsworth: Penguin Books, 1977).

8. S. Brittan, The Economic Consequences of Democracy (London: Temple Smith, 1977).

9. Manchester Guardian, June 13, 1978.

10. Steven Toulmin, "You Norman, Me Saxon," Encounter, September 1978.

11. Sir Alex Cairncross, J. A. Kay, A. Silbuston et al., "The Regeneration of Manufacturing Industry," Midland Bank Review, Autumn 1977.

12. Glynn and Sutcliffe, op. cit., p. 189.

13. Lloyd Ulman, "Collective Bargaining and Industrial Efficiency," in Britain's Economic Prospects, ed. R. E. Caves and Associates (Washington, D. C.: Brookings Institution, 1968).

14. Michael Shanks, Planning and Politics (London: George Allen and Unwin, 1976), pp. 95-96.

15. See A. Caircross et al., op. cit., p. 13.

16. See Mancur Olson, The Logic of Collective Action (Cambridge, Mass.: Harvard University Press, 1965).

17. See The United Kingdom in 1980: The Hudson Report, op cit., pp. 82-91, on the fall of relative enrollment sciences. See also, J. Allen, The British Disease (London: Institute of Economic Affairs, 1976), p. 56.

18. We refer to a series of articles arising from discussions among a distinguished group of economists. The authors of the particular article cited are R. C. O. Mathews and M. A. King.

19. R. Bacon and W. Eltis, Britain's Economic Problem: Too Few Producers, 2d ed. (London: Macmillan, 1978).

20. Ibid. , p. 100.

21. See Hennessy, Lutz, and Scimone, op. cit. , p. 72.

22. B. G. Malkiel, "The Capital Formation Problem in the U. S. ," Proceedings issue of the Journal of Finance, May 1979.

4

SWEDEN—EARLY SUCCESS AND LATER PROBLEMS

For 44 years, from 1932 to 1976, Swedened was governed by a socialist party—the Social Democrats. The coalition of the opposition parties, center and conservative, that took office in 1976 has promulgated some changes in policy emphases and a slowdown in the implementation of socialistic economic programs, but hardly a dismantling of the previous structure. In spite of, or because of the socialistic government (depending on the point of view), postwar Sweden has done considerably better than Britain in terms of per-capita income growth. However, as is true in most of the industrial world, the Swedes, of late, have experienced economic trouble. From the latter part of 1973 through the first half of 1978, there was a recession. In 1977, Sweden, Finland, and Britain were the three Western European countries who suffered a fall in real GNP; Sweden's drop of 2.5 percent was the largest. Moreover, there are many economists who believe that this recession was only symptomatic of deeper problems, and that the Swedish economy is presently overburdened with a socialist-framed redistribution system that is likely to provide considerable difficulty in the future.

At any rate, the Swedes have an advanced economy. The real per-capita income growth rate of Sweden, of about 3.3 percent per annum from 1950 to 1972, was well in excess of that of Britain, somewhat higher than that of the United States, although below that of the original Common Market six.

The relative success of socialist Sweden vis-a-vis the United Kingdom is explainable perhaps by more than one factor. The nature of the Swedes themselves may furnish one explanation. Sweden is a small country with a relatively homogeneous population of 8.5 million. In such a country, it may, for a while, be easier to obtain the unstated community sanctions upon which voluntary socialism may depend. In contrast, the population of the United Kingdom is 56 million; in addition to the native tribes of the English, Scots, Welsh, and Irish, over 4.0 percent of the population are Commonwealth immigrants, mainly from India, Pakistan, Africa, and the West Indies. (No sane observer would assume that this is the main part of the British problem.)

Schumpeter imputed the accomplishments of Swedish socialism to the special nature of Swedish society:

> Like her art, her science, her politics, her social
> institutions and much besides, her socialism and her
> socialists owe their distinction not to any peculiar
> features of principle or intention, but the stuff the
> Swedish nation is made of and to its exceptionally well-
> balanced social structure. That is why it is so absurd
> for other nations to try to copy Swedish examples; the
> only effective way of doing so would be to import the
> Swedes and to put them in charge. [1]

No doubt, part of the explanation for the Swedish economy's ability to maneuver, under a socialist superstructure, has rested on the pragmatic nature of the representatives of Swedish interest groups. The various parties (including labor) seem to have understood that the national product represented a budget constraint, and that therefore the excessive economic demands of one group would involve costs imposed on other groups. Thus, in 1978, the LO (the Swedish Federation of Labor) negotiated a base-pay increase of only 5.0 percent (although total wage costs will effectively rise about 9.5 percent after other adjustments are added). Since the rate of price-level increase was 11.4 percent in 1977 and about 11.0 percent in 1978, the labor federation accepted a slight cut in the real wage rate. This should help to restore the competitiveness of Swedish industry and strengthen the financial position of Swedish firms. Of course, it is difficult to know how long this voluntary restraint will last. Still, one may contrast this realism with the attitude of the Joan Robinson-Cambridge School, which holds that inflation is simply the result of the fight for income shares and, as such, reflects the ability of labor to resist exploitation. (This last argument follows from the Cambridge School belief that there is no allocative function for the division of income shares. In effect, higher returns will not encourage a larger capital stock, because there really is no such thing as a real stock of capital. Presumably, the relative income shares are politically or sociologically determined outside the economic system.)

At any rate, the Swedes had a good postwar run. They are

now faced with a problem of readjustment, as their economy begins to confront the high costs of transfer payments and social services that were not so evident 30 or 40 years ago, when the programs were legislated.

Let us see if we can trace some of the elements, past and present, in the Swedish situation that might be compared or contrasted with the situation in the United Kingdom. The Swedes had:

1. a strong commitment to trade and external competition;
2. profitable, exploitable natural resources: timber, iron ore, and water power;
3. no external postwar debt;
4. a central labor organization imbued with a pragmatic wage policy;
5. a pragmatic distributional system of socialism versus a programmatic commitment to the nationalization of industry;
6. a lucky hit in investment strategy;
7. a homogeneous population;
8. a wide spread of educational effort;
9. increasing participation of women in the labor force;
10. a lag before the tax-expenditure system become immoderately large.

We shall not be able to deal with all of these items in depth. We shall try to discuss briefly those that seem most important.

At the end of World War II, the GNP per capita of Sweden was somewhat below that of England. However, Sweden had no external debt comparable to the British sterling balances.

In fact, at the end of 1945, the Swedish Riksbank (central bank) was a creditor to the amount of 2.88 billion kronor (approximately $685 million at the prevailing exchange rate) in gold and net foreign claims. (Foreign debt was negligible.) In 1946, the exchange value of the kronar was raised from 23.8 cents to 27.8 cents, and wartime price controls were maintained until 1950. This policy reduced the rate of domestic inflation, but it resulted in a heavy import deficit—as large as 1.9 billion kronor in 1947. In September 1949, the kronar was devalued to approximately 19.3 cents. The effect on the trade balance was salutary; the import deficit was closed at the end of the year, and the gold and foreign exchange reserves rebounded to the level of 1.32 billion kronor.

This little synopsis of Swedish immediate postwar history should not be considered the tale of a wastrel. Much of the drawdown in the Swedish gold and reserve balance went into capital investment. At the close of the 1940s, the Swedish economy was poised to take advantage of the favorable effect on her exports of the rise in raw-material prices, induced by the Korean War.

THE ADVANTAGES OF NATURAL-RESOURCE ENDOWMENTS

In addition to her mostly intact capital stock at the end of World War II, Sweden had important natural resources. She had water power (which furnished a cheap and available supply of hydroelectric power), iron mines, and forest lands. In his comparison of the performance of British and Swedish companies, C. F. Pratten listed, as an important factor favoring the Swedes, the number of companies controlling natural resources. Such companies accounted for about 21 percent of Swedish exports, compared to only 8 percent of U. K. exports for companies with similar advantages. Moreover, cheap Swedish electric power aided the competitiveness of the Swedish steel industry.[2] Primary commodities composed 39 percent of Swedish exports in 1960 (22 percent in 1975), as against 16 percent of the U. K. exports in 1960 (and 17 percent in 1975).[3]

Swedish resource-based industries earned a considerable amount of foreign exchange over the postwar period. Favorably situated, exploitable natural resources may be peculiarly useful to a society devoted to distributional socialism. Such resources earn economic rents or surpluses. Labor and management must be rewarded to bring forth their effort, and capital must be compensated to encourage its preservation and to cover the sacrifice and the risk involved in its formation. However, since land or natural resources are already in existence, the returns from their use are a form of surplus. (Of course, a price must be developed for these resources to ensure their proper allocation to various uses over time.)* Nevertheless, it is likely that the rents from such resources can be spent on public capital or on transfer payments, without severely distorting the efficient allocation of other factors.

The Swedish natural resources constituted a net economic advantage, even though the returns from their exploitation may have been used mainly to offset allocative inefficiencies. In any case, this favored Sweden against the British performance. However, the relevant comparison for Great Britain in this area is perhaps the economic performances of West Germany and Japan. These countries' natural resources bases are surely not much better than the United

---

*The problem of natural-resource rents is more complex than is apparent at first glance. Exploration and development costs are capital investments and, as such, must be fully compensated if they are to continue to be made.

TABLE 4. 1

Sweden's Principal Commodity Exports

	Percent of Total Exports			
	1950	1960	1970	1976
Iron ore	7. 0	7. 9	3. 6	2. 4
Round wood, sawn and planed softwood	9. 5	8. 7	6. 5	4. 5
Pulp	19. 6	13. 9	7. 9	6. 8
Newsprint	1. 9	2. 0	1. 4	1. 6
Other paper and cardboard	7. 4	6. 6	6. 5	8. 0
Subtotal: wood and wood-derived products	37. 4	30. 2	22. 3	20. 9
Telephone and telegraph equipment	0. 8	1. 4	3. 5	3. 6
Office machinery	0. 8	1. 7	2. 4	1. 3
Ships and boats	6. 3	7. 0	5. 6	7. 2
Automobiles and trucks	0. 3	3. 6	8. 8	7. 0

Source: Skandinaviska Enskilda Banken, Some Facts on Sweden (Stockholm, 1977-78).

Kingdom's; nevertheless, they have made up for this by a high rate of savings and capital formation.

In contrast to the Swedish situation, the one major British resource up to now has been coal. The British coal mines (nationalized) have not provided much net support for the economy. In 1978, the English coal fields did earn a slight profit, but this was largely absorbed by the deficits incurred in keeping the Scottish and Welsh mines operating. * (Moreover, at the end of 1978, the miners were calling for a 40 percent wage raise as an opener—they apparently settled, in February 1979, for 9 percent.)

However, in Sweden too, the surge of wage costs in the recent

---

*It is believed that the newly surveyed coal fields near York have considerable economic potential.

past has taken its toll (wage costs through 1975 and 1976 rose at an annual rate of about 23 percent). Swedish forestry products are no longer as internationally competitive against the lower costs of the Canadian and Finnish industries and the output of Brazil. According to Table 4. 1, wood or wood-derived products were 38. 4 percent of Swedish exports in 1950 and 20. 9 percent in 1976. In 1977, the Swedish forestry industries were subsidized for about $350 million.

The iron mines, too, are having difficulties against foreign competition (see Table 4. 2). The Swedish share of world iron ore output fell from 7. 2 percent in 1952 to about 3. 7 percent in 1975. Iron ore was 7. 9 percent of total Swedish exports in 1960, but only 2. 4 percent in 1976.

The surge of output from Brazilian mines is displacing Swedish ore even in its customary markets in Central Europe. Current problems have led to nationalization of the mines; presently, 80 percent of the mines are state owned, as against 30 percent in 1975. But these are recent developments; for most of the postwar period, the output of Sweden's forests and mines was in strong demand. (Even in the great depression, the secular rise in the demand for paper pulp helped cushion the downturn for the Swedish economy.)

Foreign Trade and Competitive Attitudes

One salient feature of Swedish postwar economic policy has been a commitment to open trade. The rigor and discipline of competing in the international markets helped to overcome the rigidities of the domestic economy. The effect of competition was apparently also a matter of national psychology (if such things exist), with the Swedes taking pride in the quality of their products and in their ability to capture a fair share of foreign markets. * In a small, open economy, the amount of foreign trade relative to the GNP must be relatively high. The necessity of competing in foreign markets induced a sense of realism in Swedish wage demands and also inculcated a sense of managerial responsibility. It was understood that productivity would have to be high and costs controlled, if the price of Swedish exports were to be competitive.

---

*This too may, unfortunately, be in a period of change; I was told that the quality of some products was not up to previous standards. There was hope that new managements and the cold douse of the economic downturn would restore the sense of workmanship.

TABLE 4.2

World Iron Ore Production: Some Major Producers, Selected Years, 1939-76 (output in 1,000 metric tons)

Year	Sweden		Australia		Brazil		Total World Output*
	Output	Percent of World Output	Output	Percent of World Output	Output	Percent of World Output	
1939	8,360	11.5	1,727	2.4	363	0	72,700
1946	4,308	5.9	1,229	1.7	396	0.6	72,500
1955	10,452	6.0	2,334	1.3	2,300	1.3	174,700
1967	17,595	5.2	11,104	3.3	14,772	4.4	338,200
1973	22,071	4.7	47,204	10.1	37,413	8.0	468,100
1974	22,856	4.5	57,801	11.3	62,212	12.11	513,700
1975	19,642	3.9	60,860	12.0	58,431	11.51	507,500
1976	19,109	3.7	58,263	11.4	60,596	11.82	512,700

*Up till 1958; excludes China.

Note: Figures refer to the iron content of iron ores mined, including manganiferous iron ores, but excluding pyrites.

Source: United Nations Statistical Yearbook (New York: Department of International Economic and Social Affairs—Statistical Office, 1947-76).

72

SWEDISH LABOR AND THE DOCTRINE OF SOLIDARITY

As is true of British labor, Swedish labor is highly organized—about 70 percent of the labor force belong to unions. The main body of Swedish labor is organized in the federation of manual workers' unions (LO); the white-collar workers have their own organization (the TCO); and the professionals are organized in their own confederation (SACO). These organizations are generally political allies, but in 1971, the white-collar workers and professionals went on a slowdown to protest the narrowness of the pay differential between them and the unskilled—the small reward for their extra responsibility and training. Although there are some significant differences in the organization of the Swedish and the British labor markets, on one point—the narrow differential in the net pay between skilled and unskilled workers—observers note a troublesome similarity. The slim reward for skill reduces the relative supply of skilled workers. In Britain, the basic problem of this situation is revealed when the economy moves up toward fuller employment. At such times, there is an available supply of unskilled workers, but the shortage of trained and specialized workers brings about production bottlenecks, and the resulting sharply rising marginal costs tend to cut short the recovery.

One outstanding difference between British and Swedish labor organization is the power of the Swedish central unions. The Swedish central labor organization negotiates the basic annual wage bargain for the whole economy.* Moreover, contrary to England, where the TUC is loosely knit (or to Israel, where the Histadrut cannot enforce its writ), the wage agreement is pretty well enforced. Of course, the exact percentage of the wage agreement may shift up a bit because of wage drift—that is, the inclusion of adjustments and additional holidays in the wage bargain, and the tendency to promote workers more rapidly to higher classifications under conditions of a tight labor market.

One of the underlying precepts of the national wage bargain is the ideal of solidarity. Solidarity implies that in an ideal world, all workers should enjoy approximately the same income. When put into

---

*Among other devices, the employers' confederation uses something akin to a TIP (tax-incentive plan) to aid in keeping individual company settlements in line. An employer who pays higher than the agreed level may be assessed a penalty by the employers' federation. Whether this sanction is much of an effective deterrent is not clear.[4]

practice, solidarity reduces the pay differential for skill. It also means that as far as possible, workers in different industries and different firms will receive similar pay. In effect, the labor costs of weak firms or industries are pushed close to those of the strong firms or industries. Although the concept appears startling at first, the economy can function under this policy as long as the wage settlement allows the export sector to remain competitive, and as long as the labor market is sufficiently mobile to allow easy shifting of the labor force. For in fact, one feature of the theoretical equilibrium in a pure competitive labor market is that the price of labor would be the same for all employers. (If there were any disequilibrium, the more efficient producers would hire more labor up to the point where wages equaled marginal productivity, and the less well situated firms would release that part of their labor force whose wage was in excess of productivity at the margin.)* In the actual case, the solidarity rule put pressure on the less efficient or less competitive sectors of the Swedish economy. Firms which could not compete at the going labor costs might be forced to liquidate entirely or, at least, to reduce the scale of their operations. In simpler terms, they had to lay off some of their employees. [5]

Apparently the workers were willing to bear the sacrifices that the implementation of solidarity entailed. The costs of the solidarity program impinge on labor incomes in several guises. Social security funds are used to pay the salaries and the retraining and relocation costs of the workers who are made redundant in the less efficient industries. The necessarily high social security taxes reduce the net take-home pay of the employed workers.

Another effect of the program is to raise the costs and the prices of nontraded, domestic goods and services, because the general wage-cost level is set by the productivity-leading export industries. Thus the high ranking given Swedish per-capita income, when the translation is made on the basis of international exchange rates, becomes a bit less favorable when the incomes are deflated by prevailing domestic price levels.

The policy of solidarity brings about a concentration of employment in the growth sectors, and the necessity of speedy relocation for workers in the lagging industries. This requires deliberate policy, for in its natural state, the labor market is not completely mobile in

---

*In the mobile competitive model, the equality of wages is due to the working out of several forces. On the supply side, the workers themselves would move from lower- to higher-paying industries until wages and marginal products were equal in all industries.

the short run (nor need it be if all costs and human preferences are counted). The welfare question that needs asking is: Should a worker in a declining or less competitive industry be prohibited from settling for a relatively lower wage if, out of personal preference, he prefers to remain at his present position?[6]

The policy of industry wage equality has the effect of enforcing economic efficiency in the use of labor. It apparently can work as long as the wage costs in the export industries are reasonable, so that their prices are internationally competitive, and as long as aggregate demand in the whole economy is buoyant enough to absorb the workers displaced from other industries. The result of this economic mobility may be to concentrate more of the economic activity in the lead industries. *

The other side of the coin involves the willingness to take losses and reshift the economic base if the lead industries should lose their competitive edge. This willingness to pay the social cost of mobility was somewhat dampened at the end of the 1960s and has not been strongly demonstrated in the present crisis. To quote Eric Lundberg:

> The stern rationalization and structural transformation process in business and industry dealt in many instances harshly with certain categories of manpower, primarily older people and unskilled workers. Pockets of unemployment appeared in stagnating areas. The mobility policy proved to have limited possibilities of solving this problem. It became more and more apparent that the high productivity gains of the 1960's was being purchased at the cost of sacrifices in human welfare, concentrated to the groups mentioned. They were subjected to unemployment, retraining, geographical transfers, early retirement, low incomes—even the objective of income equalization was in danger. . . .
>
> From the end of the 1960's, labor policy has shifted more and more from activities designed to increase mobility toward those intended to preserve and stimulate

---

*It has been argued that mobility worked because in a small economy, a few lucky investments in the portfolio of real capital may provide a considerable drive for growth. This has been forwarded as a possible explanation of Sweden's growth until the recent slowdown. Of course, this argument might be weighed against the fact that most of Europe—small and large countries alike—did well in the postwar world.

employment at the local level, in the individual firm, and within the region. [7]

But at least up to the 1970s, the Swedish commitment to efficiency in the use of labor, and to the consequent necessity of relocating redundant workers, contrasts with the British tendency of trying to maintain the employment of workers where they are.

Educational Effort

The Swedes have shown a greater willingness or ability, than have the British, to provide higher education in general, and higher technical education in particular, to a larger portion of the population. According to the OECD, on the basis of relevant age groups, the Swedes have 31 percent enrolled in higher learning; the British, 22 percent; and the Americans, 43 percent. Table 4.3 gives the data over time, on the basis of total population. * While in no way comparable to the American effort, the Swedes enroll a considerably higher percentage of their population, than do the British, in institutions of higher education. Moreover, a higher percentage of the students take courses in applied areas; this provides Swedish engineering and business with a broader cadre of trained personnel than that available to British industry. The cult of amateurism that is supposed to pervade British administration is presumably not prevalent in Swedish industry.

The Degree of Nationalization

An additional important factor in the comparison between the two economies is the degree of public ownership. Up until recently, somewhat less than 5 percent of Swedish industry was governmentally owned; over 10 percent of British industry was publicly owned. Recent setbacks in the economy have forced the Swedish government into the major ownership of the failing steel conglomerate, and into picking up additional iron ore mines to go with the workings inherited at the end of the nineteenth century. However, up to now, the Swedes, for

---

*Again, we make the proviso: the cardinal data may not always be directly comparable, because the definition of higher education across countries is not always the same. (Part of the apparent discrepancy between the data of the OECD and Table 4.3 is due to the fact that higher education lasts three years in England and Sweden, four years in the United States.) However, the ordinal rankings are correct.

TABLE 4.3

Number of University Students per 1,000
of Total Population

Country	1940	1950	1960	1970	1975
Sweden	1.7	2.3	5.0	14.3	14.2
United Kingdom:					
England and Wales	1.1	2.3	2.7	5.1	5.2
United States	11.3	17.6	17.9	35.1	42.2

Sources: United Nations, Statistical Yearbook (New York, 1976); Bureau of the Budget, Statistical Abstract of the United States (Washington, D.C.: Government Printing Office, 1977).

the most part, have been relieved of the dilemma of wrestling with the extra objectives often imposed on nationalized industries—whether they are to be run as employers of last resort, to relieve incipient unemployment; and/or whether their product is to be sold below cost, as an incentive to other industries or as a boon to certain deserving classes of consumers.

SOME ASPECTS OF THE BACON-ELTIS ANALYSIS
APPLIED TO SWEDEN

The ideological core of the Swedish system is not the national-ization of capital or wealth, but distributional socialism. In essence, market-generated incomes are to be redistributed by a comprehen-sive system of transfer payments. * This involves cradle-to-the-grave security—a pervasive network of government payments and subsidies for medical care, housing, income security and job re-training; nursery schools, education, and pensions. As can be seen

---

*Only on the surface does the Swedish system differ from a redistribution of wealth. In the Fisherian sense, where wealth is the present value of a future flow of income, the redistribution of income is the equivalent of a redistribution of wealth.

TABLE 4. 4

Total Public Expenditures as Percent of
Gross Domestic Product at Market Prices

Country	1965	1970	1975	1977
Germany	37	38	48	47
Norway	34	43	50	51
Sweden	35	43	52	62
United Kingdom	37	41	50	44
United States	27	32	35	33

Source: O. E. C. D.

from Table 4. 4, the system has grown to the point where 62 percent
of the Swedish GNP is now taken up by the government sector.

Tables 4. 4-4. 6 illustrate the application of the Bacon and Eltis
analysis to the Swedish situation. The growth rate of the Swedish
nonmarket sector exceeded that of the United Kingdom over the period
1965 to 1975, although the absolute amount of per-capita GNP re-
maining in the market sector still was larger than that in the United
Kingdom. At any rate, the impact of the nonmarket sector's take on
the market-sector output is now higher in Sweden than in Great
Britain. The crossing point was somewhere in the late 1960s—the
exact point depending on the measure used. However, the relatively
high level of Swedish output in the 1960s and the prevailing high level
of savings and capital investment gave the economy a forward velocity that, for a time, was able to sustain the tremendous increase in
the government sector. But, the structure of the economy changed.
During the period 1960 to 1975, total employment grew by about
420, 000. However, employment in forestry, fishing, and agriculture
declined by 320, 000; manufacturing employment held about steady;
and service-industry employment increased by about 110, 000. The
net drop in employment of 210, 000, in the other sectors, plus the
natural increase in the work force was absorbed by employment in
the government sector, which rose by 570, 000 jobs.

The rate of consumption from market-generated income
actually declined by . 49 percent per annum from 1965 to 1975. (The
English economy did slightly better; the rate of private-consumption

TABLE 4.5

Comparison of the Relative Impact of the Nonmarket Sectors,
Sweden and the United Kingdom, Selected Years, 1955-75

Year	Nonmarket Sector Purchases of Marketed Output as a Proportion of Marketed Output (Including Defense Expenditures)		Proportion of Personal Income Derived from Nonmarket Sector (Excluding Defense Expenditures)	
	Britain	Sweden	United Kingdom	Sweden
1955	31.5	30.2	26.4	20.9
1965	30.5	36.7	26.2	28.7
1974	35.9	47.9	30.2	43.7
1975	36.9	48.2	32.0	44.49

Sources: Robert Bacon and Walter Eltis, Britain's Economic
Problem: Too Few Producers (London: Macmillan, 1976); Swedish
Central Bureau of Statistics, "National Income Accounts" (Stockholm,
1955-75).

growth out of market-generated incomes was 0.60 percent per annum
over this period.) The present increase in Swedish labor absentee-
ism, slowdowns, and demands for longer vacations lends credence
to the Bacon and Eltis hypothesis that a likely result of high marginal
tax rates and a low rate of growth of private discretionary consumption is an "internal migration" away from paid employment. [8]
Perhaps at this point, we might note a few truths about transfer
payments and pension payments in particular. After a certain level
of social services is reached, socialistic redistribution can hardly
be based on the transfer of income from the rich to the poor. The
massive social security arrangements in such countries as Sweden
rest on minimally better-off persons' paying for social services to
the poor and the retired. Essentially, the system is financed by
labor's supporting its own benefits. Moreover, the full effect of the
redistribution means that there is little additional reward, after
taxes and payroll contributions, for superior skill, talents, entrepreneurship, risk taking, or education. It is likely that as of the

TABLE 4.6

Swedish Growth Rates in Market Output, and In Market and
Nonmarket Consumption and Investment, 1955-75

Growth Item	1955-65	1965-75	1955-75
Annual growth rate in real output of market sector	3.83%	2.56%	3.19%
Annual growth rate in market output remaining in market sector	2.81	.52	1.66
Annual growth rate in real market output invested and consumed by nonmarket sector	5.89	5.39	5.64
Annual growth rate in real market output consumed privately from market-generated income	2.12	-.49	.81

Source: Calculated from Swedish Central Bureau of Statistics, "National Income Accounts" (Stockholm, 1955-75).

present, the Swedish manager receives an even lower real take-home, private-goods wage than does his British counterpart. [9] (Of course, as we have noted before, such a comparison does not count the imputed value of the government services that are provided free. These services, however, are not distributed in a manner which parallels the value of an individual's productive contribution—nor his or her consumption preferences.)

Looking into the future, one may fear a further adverse impact of the social security contributions on the real take-home pay of the employed worker. When the financial facade is removed, it is obvious that the purchasing power of pension payments derives from the active labor force's sharing its output with the retired. (Money in itself is not much use; there has to be an output of goods and services for the elderly to buy.) The burden of the pension system is low when there is a growing supply of labor relative to the retirees. Under these circumstances, the percentage of incomes that will have to be paid into the pension funds will not appear burdensome. However, the weight of the pension system becomes heavier when the number of pensioners increases relative to the active labor force. (Those who think that affirmative-action fairness for the childless worker calls

FIGURE 4.1

Population Pyramids

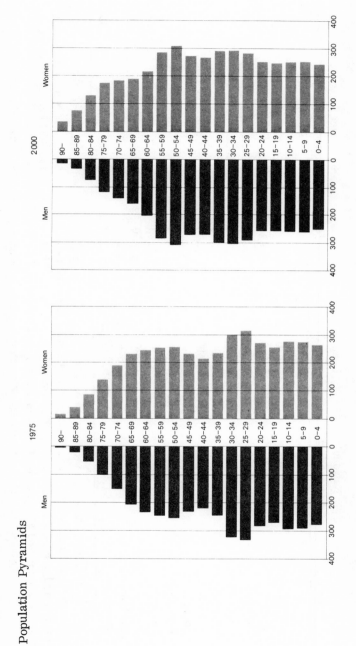

Note: The left pyramid shows the population situation in 1975; the right one is a year-2000 projection, assuming no net migration; persons in different age groups, 1,000.

Source: Skandinaviska Enskilda Banken, Some Facts on Sweden (Stockholm, 1978).

81

TABLE 4.7

Swedish Aggregate National and Local Income Taxes for Individuals, 1977

Annual Gross Income (kronor)	National Income Tax	Local Income Tax	Total Tax	Tax as Percentage of Income	Marginal Tax Rate on Added Income (percent)
5,000	—	—	—	—	29
20,000	50	4,030	4,080	20.4	31
25,000	250	5,370	5,620	22.5	33
30,000	550	6,710	7,260	24.2	37
35,000	1,050	8,060	9,110	26.0	42
40,000	1,800	9,400	11,200	28.0	48
45,000	3,100	10,740	13,840	30.8	53
50,000	4,400	12,080	16,840	33.0	62
65,000	9,800	16,110	25,910	39.9	65
70,000	11,700	17,450	29,150	41.6	70
75,000	13,850	18,800	32,650	43.5	75
105,000	28,450	26,850	55,300	52.7	80
155,000	54,950	40,280	95,230	61.4	85

Note: The table applies to income earned during 1977 by persons who were taxable in Sweden in 1978. Average local income tax is 26.85 percent. The calculation takes into account expense deductions totaling 500 kronor and personal allowance, 4,500. When the gross income in in excess of 155,000 kronor, the tax is 95,230 kronor and 85 percent of the remainder.

Source: Skandinaviska Enskilda Banken, Some Facts on Sweden (Stockholm, 1978).

for the elimination of family benefits for workers with children should
have second thoughts. If there is no future generation, there will be
no pensions.) At any rate, Figure 4.1, which shows an inverse pyramid for the age profile of the Swedish population, foretells trouble
ahead. The number of new entrants to the labor force is falling off,
and the number of retirements is increasing. The population is aver-
aging a greater age. In 1977, for the first time, deaths exceeded
births by a small amount.

INCREASE IN FEMALE PARTICIPATION
IN THE LABOR FORCE, AND
ITS EFFECT ON GNP

The Swedish welfare and tax system has led to a high rate of
female participation in the market labor force. This leads to a relative overstatement of the Swedish per-capita GNP, compared to the
United States and Great Britain (in addition to the bias induced by
higher domestic prices). Let me explain. Since 1968, the Swedish
tax system has made no concessions for single-income families. As
can be seen from Table 4.7, the average worker making a good wage
of about 60,000 kronor a year (about $13,500) is subject to a mar-
ginal tax rate of 60 percent—perhaps more if account is taken of the
legal reduction of various subsidies and allowances when one reaches
this level. However, if his wife goes to work, her earnings are taxed
as an independent income. If she brings in an additional 30,000
kronor (about $6,600), it is taxed at a 37 percent rate; if the husband
were to work harder and add this same amount to his wages or salary, the incremental tax would come to about 66 2/3 percent, or
20,000 kronor ($4,300); the family would net only 10,000 kronor
($2,200) for his effort. (The American system, which contains a
split-income provision, or the U.K. system, which allows relatively
high dependent deductions, do not quite have this effect.)

As might be expected, the effect of such a tax system is to
urge women into the labor markets. A high proportion of Swedish
women have entered the labor market in recent years. Some 42 percent of Swedish women are currently in the labor force, a considerably higher rate of participation than in the United Kingdom or the
United States (see Table 4.8). Taking another view of this development, over the period 1960 to 1970, the Swedish population grew at
the rate of 0.7 percent, whereas the labor force grew at the considerably higher rate of 1 percent (see Table 4.9). This helped raise
national income per capita, because when a larger proportion of the
population is at work, total output per capita is higher even if there
is little or no increase in productivity per worker. In the United

TABLE 4. 8

Percentage of Female Population in the Work Force,
and Females as a Percentage of the Work Force

Year	Sweden	United Kingdom	United States
		Percentage	
1955*	25. 2	28. 2	24. 5
1965	29. 8	32. 3	27. 0
1975	42. 0	33. 8	33. 9
		Females	
1955	27. 4	31. 4	30. 1
1965	33. 6	34. 8	34. 0
1975	42. 4	37. 6	39. 1

*1955 percentages are interpolated from 1953–57
data.
Sources: International Labor Organization, Year-
book of Labor Statistics (Geneva: ILO, various issues);
Statistical Office, Annual Abstract of Statistics (London:
Her Majesty's Stationery Office, various issues).

Kingdom, over this period, the growth in the labor force just kept
pace with the population growth. However, for both the United States
and Sweden, a considerable part of the difference between population
growth and labor-force growth is explained by the increased entry
of women into the labor force. (Another factor making for a discrepancy between the labor-force growth and population growth would be
the changing age composition of the population.)

The high rate of Swedish female participation in the labor
force increases the relative GNP in still another, and perhaps more
basic, manner. In standard national-income accounting, the output
in goods or services of the market-paid female worker is counted in
the total, whereas the value of services performed domestically is
omitted. (One is reminded of the legendary economist who refused
to marry his housekeeper because it would reduce the GNP.) Moreover, families with two workers tend to generate a demand for such

TABLE 4.9

Comparison of the Annual Percentage Rates of Growth
of the Population and the Work Force: Sweden, the
United Kingdom, and the United States, 1960-70

Country	Per-Annum Growth Rate, Total Population, 1960-70	Per-Annum Growth Rate, Labor Force, 1960-70
United Kingdom	0.6	0.6
Sweden	0.7	1.0
United States	1.2	1.8

Source: World Bank, World Development Report,
1978 (Washington, D.C.: World Bank, August 1978).

goods and services as nursery schools, restaurant meals, social
service workers, and part-time household work. These items, which
are counted as part of the national income, are, however, substitutes
in an economic sense for nonaccountable domestic services performed by housekeepers.

To obtain a true measure of comparative national incomes, it
would be necessary to net out the value of domestic services displaced by the entry of women into the labor market. It might be dis-
covered that the actual net social product contributed by many women
workers is negligible. Russian economists once calculated that if the
average woman worker had to place two or more children in nursery
school, then, in general, the total incremental social costs cancelled
out her earnings.[10] Peculiarly enough, many of the new women
workers are employed in the service fields, especially in the public
sector. As Table 4.10 shows, there is heavy employment of women
in such occupations as children's nurse and cleaner. These are close
substitutes for domestic output.

Not everyone is pleased by a tax system that prejudices family
arrangements in favor of working wives. The effect is to dampen the
incentives of the main income earner to increase his skills and output. It impels the wife into the labor market (and forces her to purchase external domestic services) even if she should prefer the more
conventional division of labor. At any rate, the accelerated rate of

TABLE 4.10

Occupations with More Than 10,000 Women in Sweden

Occupation	Number of Women	Percent Women in the Occupation
Shop assistant	127,898	80
Secretary, typist	74,592	96
Farmer	62,351	54
Cleaner	57,346	91
Nurse's aide	56,381	98
Maid, child's nurse	52,221	100
Special office employee	50,713	68
Clerical assistant	36,422	82
Sewer	35,909	98
Bookkeeper, cashier	35,909	98
Waitress	28,884	89
Teacher (grades 1-6)	27,980	75
Nurse	25,658	100
Kitchen assistant	24,904	95
Telephone operators	21,497	99
Shopkeeper	18,905	29
Hairdresser	17,728	74
Home helper	17,578	100
Textile worker	14,352	55
Cook	13,960	82
Cattleman	13,206	73
Packing man	12,603	66
Lab technician	11,517	57
Cashier	11,337	98
Home economist	10,583	77
Total	860,163	
Women in other fields	105,364	

Source: Nancy S. Barret, "Have Swedish Women Achieved Equality?" Challenge, November-December 1973.

Swedish female labor-force participation (although, of course, it cannot explain the whole difference) accounts for some of the gap between Swedish and British per-capita bookkeeping GNP. It probably explains a significant part of Sweden's accounting GNP growth rate from 1960 to 1970.

The Tax System and the Second Economy

Depending on the speaker, the Swedish tax system may be either blamed or praised for changing the family structure. On the other hand, the high marginal tax rates are almost universally blamed for encouraging the creation of a second or hidden economy. This is a sector where goods and services are bartered so as to avoid the bite of the tax collector. Very simply, a television-shop owner may give a television set to the dentist in payment for his dental work, or a plumber may pay for his car repairs by working on the garage mechanic's cottage. It is estimated that about 10 percent of the true GNP is carried out in the hidden sector, and that the taxes avoided by these second-economy activities would amount to about 7 percent of the total revenues now collected. [11]

The effect of the behavior, induced by the tax system, on the morals of the people is a matter of some concern. Gunnar Myrdal sadly observes that the high tax rates have made his people "a nation of hustlers."[12] (Also, Aron Katsenelinboigen of the University of Moscow and the University of Pennsylvania, has told me that the second economy is a most notable feature of the Soviet Union's economic structure. Apparently, this type of behavior is likely to be elicited by any heavy arbitrary interference with the normal workings of supply and demand.)

STRUCTURAL PROBLEMS AND MONETARY POLICY

Recently, the economic performance of Sweden has begun to falter; many problems have begun to surface, and anomalies in the system have become more apparent. The current Swedish problems, which include, symptomatically, such developments as work actions, high concealed unemployment, a slowdown in the economic growth rate, and the development of the second economy, may be a sign that the Swedish string is beginning to run out. One hears talk among businessmen and economists that the Swedes have caught the "English disease."

The Swedish economists are becoming aware that the redistributive policies may have a dampening effect on pure economic efficiency. Apparently, up until the early 1960s, the redistributive

TABLE 4.11

The Economic Structure of Five Industrial Nations

Country	Proportion Spent on Total Public Current Expenditure (Excluding Transfer Payments)		Proportion Spent on Total Public Current Expenditure (Including Transfer Payments)		Proportion Produced by the Manufacturing Sector		Proportion Spent on Gross Domestic Fixed Capital Formation
	1972	Increase, 1961–72	1972	Increase, 1961–72	1972	Increase, 1961–72	Annual Average 1961–72
United Kingdom	20.7%	+2.7%	41.9%	+7.9%	30.1%	-3.6%	19.8%
France	14.0	-0.7	43.1	+3.3	n.a.	n.a.	28.0
West Germany	20.4	+4.9	44.8	+4.4	47.0	-0.2	28.9
Sweden	25.6	+8.1	45.3	+15.4	27.6	-1.9	24.6
United States	23.2	+2.3	35.0	+3.7	27.5	-2.9	18.8

Source: OECD, "National Accounts, 1961–72" (Paris: OECD, 1961–73).

burden did not rest too heavily on the Swedes. It was not until 1965, when Swedish public expenditures reached 35 percent of the GNP (now 63 percent of the GNP), that this percentage exceeded that of Great Britain.

A large part of the Swedish government tax take was designated for unemployment compensation, for job retraining, and for pensions. The impact of these programs, relative to the currently produced output, does not seem heavy as long as employment is steady and the labor force is growing. Simply put, the amount required from each active worker to support the retirees is not very large, as long as the number of retirees is relatively small compared to the active labor force, or, from the viewpoint of dynamics, the number of new retirees is smaller than the number of new entrants into the labor force. Of course, it is just this ease, in a growing economy, of defer-ring the fiscal impact that lures politicians into promising generous pension and unemployment benefits in lieu of immediate pay raises. When, however, the number of new young people entering the labor force begins to decline, then the pension contributions, as a percent-age of wages, must rise if the pension fund is to be fiscally solvent. Bacon has said that Swedish labor was bought off by job-security arrangements during Sweden's growth period. Presumably, the account is now coming due. (The situation is analogous to the gener-ous pension arrangements made with American municipal workers during the 1960s and 1970s; the future level of the pension payments is likely to prove an onerous fiscal burden for years to come.)

As long as there was steady growth in the labor force and in employment, and some profitable growth industries, the Swedish tax take still left sufficient funds for private and public saving and capital formation. There was still enough net left to encourage enterprise. Moreover, the various subsidies for the payment and retraining of displaced workers came mostly out of general taxes, which, while they reduced the take-home real income derived from employment or personal investments, did not throw the burden of maintaining idle workers directly on the profitability of capital. As Table 4. 11 shows, despite the increase in the transfer-payment budget, over the period 1961-72, some 24. 6 percent of the national income was put into gross fixed capital formation. This exceeded the rate of capital formation in the United States or the United Kingdom. But in fact, the state-run pension and insurance funds were themselves a major source of investment financing; these funds are, however, no longer growing. Moreover, as will be discussed later, the profita-bility of capital investment has been declining.

As has been true of the United Kingdom and the United States, the Swedish political-economic authorities have relied upon an in-crease in the monetary base to help pull the economy through its

TABLE 4. 12

Swedish Money Supply Growth and Inflation,
1960-69 and 1970-75

Variable	Average of Annual Percentage Change	
	1960-69	1970-75
Growth in money supply*	8. 5	10. 2
Growth of real GNP	4. 3	2. 8
Annual consumer-price change	3. 9	8. 1

*Cash balances of the public, plus demand and
time deposits in commercial banks, savings banks,
the farmers' savings associations, and the Post Office
Bank (M_3).
Sources: International Monetary Fund, International Financial Statistics (Washington, D. C. : IMF,
1960-75) and Organization for Economic Cooperation
and Development, Economic Surveys: Sweden (Paris:
OECD, 1968-78).

structural difficulties. They counted on the magic of the Phillips
curve tradeoff to help sustain employment in the face of the growing
rigidities being built into the relations between wages, productivity,
and profits. To explain, the original Phillips curve was a simple
historical correlation, using U. K. statistics, showing that during
years of rising wages, employment also rose. [13] (A simple explanation might be that when the demand for labor is strong, there
tends to be an increase in both wages and employment.) A modified
version of the Phillips curve was developed which further showed
that, historically, in years of rising prices, unemployment was low.
(Presumably, during periods of strong demand for commodities
(high prices), the derived demand for productive factors—labor—
would also be strong.) This has led to the peculiar notion of the
Phillips curve policy tradeoff; that is, if the policy-makers select
some moderate level of price inflation, they can hold the level of
unemployment to a socially desirable minimum.
    However, as shown in Table 4. 12, by the 1970s, the accelerated

TABLE 4.13

Money Growth and Price-Level Changes, and Unemployment, Selected Years, 1946-77

Year	M_1 Money Stock (in billions of kronor)[a]	Annual Percent Rate of Growth of Money Stock, M_1 over the Period	Income Velocity of Money Supply, M_1 (GDP/money stock)	Annual Percent Rate of Change in Consumer Prices over the Period	Unemployment Rate (percent)[b]
1946	5.60	—	5.4X	—	—
1949	6.42	4.2	6.1	3.1	—
1953	7.41	2.6	5.9	6.3	—
1955	7.26	1.1	7.0	2.0	—
1958	7.98	3.2	7.8	4.4	—
1961	10.72	10.3	7.3	2.4	2.0
1964	13.91	9.1	7.4	3.7	2.3
1967	17.14	7.2	7.7	5.3	3.2
1970	17.17	1.2	9.6	6.8	5.2
1973	23.05	9.1	9.6	6.8	5.2
1974	28.83	25.0	8.6	9.9	4.4
1975	31.36	8.8	9.1	9.8	3.8
1976	33.48	6.8	9.6	10.3	4.2
1977	36.22	8.2	9.6	11.4	5.7

[a]M_1 money stock equals demand deposits and currency in circulation.
[b]Includes the unemployed, relief work, retraining, and protected employment; does not include the partly unemployed (OECD data).

Sources: International Monetary Fund, International Financial Statistics (Washington, D. C.: IMF, 1977); International Labor Organization, Yearbook of Labor Statistics (Geneva: ILO, 1977).

TABLE 4.14

Sweden: Growth in Money Stock—M_2, Selected Years, 1946-77

Year	M_2 Money Stock (in billions of kronor)*	Annual Percent Rate of Growth of Money Stock, M_2 over the Period	Income Velocity of M_2 (GDP/M_2)
1946	11.04	—	2.8X
1949	13.86	7.9	2.9
1953	16.86	5.0	2.6
1955	17.94	3.2	2.8
1958	22.25	7.5	2.8
1961	27.26	7.0	2.9
1964	35.86	9.6	2.9
1967	45.34	8.1	3.0
1970	54.90	6.6	3.1
1973	78.97	12.9	2.9
1974	102.59	29.9	2.4
1975	114.35	11.5	2.5
1976	117.45	2.7	2.8
1977	126.78	7.9	2.8

*M_2 money stock includes demand deposits, currency in circulation, and time deposits.

Source: International Monetary Fund, International Financial Statistics (Washington, D.C.: IMF, 1977).

growth in the Swedish money supply, M_2 (defined as currency in circulation, demand deposits and time deposits), began to produce considerable price level increases whereas the increase in real income was moderate. Table 4.13 shows the behavior of other economic variables relative to the course of the M_1 money stock. During the 1970s the velocity or turnover rate of the M_1 money supply rose compared to previous periods. However, the velocity of M_2 balances, which include interest-paying savings accounts (Friedman's preferred measure), remained remarkably stable. (See Table 4.14.)

Tables 4.13 and 4.14 detail the rate of change in the Swedish money supply and changes in the price level and the level of employment from 1946 to 1977. As previously noted, the increase in money supply generated price increases and very little growth in output. In the latter part of this period, the rate of unemployment appeared to become stubbornly unamenable to monetary policy.

Thus from the view of the economic policy makers, the expansionary monetary policy of the 1970s seemed to produce some diabolically strange results. The rate of inflation accelerated, but there was little decrease in the level of unemployment. Structural rigidities asserted themselves in the form of the Friedman natural rate of unemployment—that is, the rate around which the level of unemployment seems to stick after a while regardless of the rate of inflation.[14] (Of course, there is nothing natural about this rate. It could be reduced by decreasing the rigidities in the wage structure.) In any case, on the basis of U. K. and Swedish experience, one might conclude that the Phillips tradeoff does not appear to work over any appreciable run of time. (The U. S. experience is similar.) Apparently, once the juncture is reached where the inflation rate is fully anticipated, further increases in the money supply raise the price level but make for little change in the rate of output or the reduction in the level of unemployment.

We might note one further item. The nominal interest rate does not necessarily fall with an increase in the money supply. According to the International Monetary Fund statistics, the market yield on Swedish government bonds went from 3. 06 percent in 1946 to 9. 74 percent in 1977.

Producing for Stock

In 1974, the worldwide rise in commodity prices and the fall in total world demand impinged on the Swedish economy. Nevertheless, in spite of falling international incomes, the proper thing to do, at least from the Swedish labor unions' point of view, was to raise the nominal wage to offset rising prices and to maintain the real wage. The potential effects on employment were disregarded. The wage settlements for 1975-76 raised wages about 17 percent to 18 percent per annum and labor costs about 23 percent. In the course of events, Swedish exports fell off and aggregate domestic demand dropped.

However, an interesting fiscal-policy device was instituted to cover over the downturn; Swedish firms were paid a subsidy for producing for inventory as long as they maintained the level of employment. As a result, production remained relatively high, but the government paid for what, in other times, might be called unintended investment in inventory. This accumulation of inventory maintained

TABLE 4.15

Sweden's Balance of Trade and Change in Stocks, 1965-76

Year	Current Balance: Exports Minus Imports* (millions of kronor)	Increase in Stocks	Increase in Stocks as a Percent of GNP
1965	-881	2,831	2.4
1966	-780	1,434	1.2
1967	-29	143	0.1
1968	-190	422	0.3
1969	-511	1,864	1.2
1970	-8,757	4,812	2.8
1971	-1,971	1,798	1.0
1972	2,594	-136	(0.0)
1973	6,659	-1,252	(0.6)
1974	-2,039	5,398	2.2
1975	-3,704	8,287	2.9
1976	-6,579	7,514	2.3

*Includes services, tourism, etc.

Source: Organization for Economic Cooperation and Development, Economic Surveys: Sweden (Paris: OECD, 1968-78).

the nominal GNP and, in effect, concealed the true rate of unemployment. The unemployed worked to produce inventories.

The Swedish economists were hopeful that the world recession would be short-lived. In the boom that would follow, the inventories could be sold off and normal output for current demand could be resumed. Unfortunately, the level of recovery did not move up at the rate, nor in the time period, expected. In the meantime, the refusal to adjust real costs upward and real income downward surfaced in the to-be-expected manner; large deficits appeared in the Swedish balance of payments.

As can be seen in Tables 4.14 and 4.15, the deficits in the balance of payments paralleled the amount of production for stock. In 1976, the accumulation of inventory was 7.5 billion kronor (about $1.65 billion) and the deficit in the payments balance for the year was 6.579 billion kronor (about $1.5 billion). In effect, this policy meant that work on inventory, designed to maintain domestic employment and real income, was supported by borrowing from abroad. This was not likely to last indefinitely.

CAPITAL MARKETS—LESS PROFITS, MORE DEBT

The anomalies and difficulties that surfaced in the mid-1970s showed up as forewarning symptoms in the financial and business sector of the economy. Profitability, properly measured as the ratio of profits, plus interest, over the total assets of the firm, plummeted to 3. 9 percent in 1976 and to below 1. 0 percent in 1977. (See Table 4. 16 and Figure 4. 2.) Again, as in the United States and Great Britain, the fall in profitability was somewhat papered over on the financial level through the increased use of leverage. The ratio of equity to total assets—called solidity in Swedish financial parlance*—fell from 44. 8 percent in 1967 to 34. 1 percent in 1976. † Nevertheless, in spite of the increased use of leverage, the return on equity was below the average rate being paid on long-term debt in 1975, 1976, and 1977. (Moreover, the interest rate on current debt would, of course, be even higher than the average or imbedded interest rate, which is the weighted average of the contractual rate on old debt.)

---

*The solidity ratio may be stated in two ways, either on the book-value basis, or as a higher ratio when the equity figures include the governmental reserves. These governmental reserves consist of extra tax monies withheld from the firm in good times, which may be made available to the firm for investment or other uses during economic downturns. This is supposed to be a macroeconomic stabilizing device that operates to reduce capital investments in booms and increase them during downturns. One may doubt its efficacy. During booms, the firms treat the reserves as deferred equity and use them to support increased debt; they can draw on the funds in a downturn to help cover financial deficits. However, the notion that firms will draw on the reserves during slowdowns to finance investments places too much weight on liquidity factors, and not enough on expected profitability as far as the investment decision is concerned.

†The equity level of British firms fell from 57. 5 percent in 1961 to 40. 9 percent in 1976. The Federal Trade Commission data for the United States show a similar trend; the equity ratio of U. S. nonfinancial firms fell from 58. 7 percent in 1965 to 51. 7 percent in 1977.

TABLE 4.16

Rate of Return on Capital and Financial Structures, Listed Swedish Companies, 1965-76 (Excluding Banks) (in percentages)

Year	Return after Tax on Adjusted Equity (Alternative 1)[a]	Return after Tax on Adjusted Equity (Alternative 2)[b]	Net Return before Tax, Plus Interest, over Total Adjusted Assets	Adjusted Solidity (Equity to Total Assets) (Alternative 2)	Interest Payments on Long-Term Debt (Imbedded Interest)
1965	9.0	6.0	6.5	—	—
1966	6.5	4.0	5.0	0	—
1967	6.0	3.5	4.5	44.8	6.4
1968	7.5	5.0	5.6	43.0	6.4
1969	8.8	6.0	6.6	41.7	7.0
1970	8.2	5.5	6.2	40.5	7.7
1971	6.4	4.3	4.9	39.0	7.6
1972	6.8	4.2	4.8	38.2	7.5
1973	11.3	6.9	6.8	37.2	7.9
1974	12.1	7.3	7.6	36.4	9.1
1975	6.8	4.0	5.2	35.5	9.6
1976	4.0	2.4	3.9	34.1	9.8

[a]Alternative 1—visible equity plus 50 percent of untaxed reserves.

[b]Alternative 2—equity has been adjusted to include 50 percent of untaxed reserves and estimated hidden reserves in real estate, and half of the estimated hidden reserves in machinery and inventories.

Source: Torsten Carlsson, "The Future of the Stock Market," Skandinaviska Enskilda Banken Quarterly Review, January-February 1978.

FIGURE 4.2

Earnings as a Percentage of Employed Capital for Listed Swedish
Companies, and the Trend of Interest Rates on Borrowed Capital

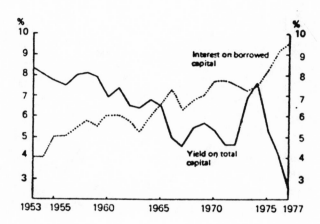

Source: Torsten Carlsson, "The Future of the Stock Market,"
Skandinaviska Enskilda Banken Quarterly Review, January-February
1978.

As is well known to students of finance, the use of debt financing can lead to an enhancement of ownership profits in normal times.
It does, however, increase financial risk and the possibility of bankruptcy. And in fact, there has been a rise in financial shortfalls in
Swedish industries in the last few years. The steel companies were
saved from failure by government takeover and financial support,
and Volvo was supposed to be either combined with Saab or rescued
by an infusion of Norwegian oil money. The effect of an increasing
trend of higher leverage ratios on the general economy is not entirely
clear, but there is considerable belief that the resulting increase in
borrowers' and lenders' risk (using Keynes's terminology) would
lead to a dampening of capital formation. [15]

FIGURE 4.3

Investment Ratio and Savings Ratio—Total Gross Investment,
Including Inventories, and Total Gross Saving as a Percentage
of GDP in Current Prices

Note: According to the national accounts, financial saving is
defined as the difference between a sector's gross saving and its
gross investment (including inventory changes).
Source: Erik Lundberg, "Stabilization Policy, Inflation and
Profits," Skandinaviska Enskilda Banken Quarterly Review, February-March 1979.

The reduction in the rate of return on capital and the increasing
risk in the financial structures of the firms have, as would be expected, indeed lowered the real rate of capital formation. This is
illustrated in Figure 4.3, which shows investment falling from a
rate of about 25 percent in 1971 to around 18 percent in 1978. The
fall in the rate of savings over this period is even greater; the difference is covered by government deficits, which, however, bring with
them the risk of accelerating inflation.

In the early 1960s, the government administered pension funds embarked on the purchase of common shares. These purchases over time have considerably reduced the floating supply of equity securities on the stock market. The participants in the private-capital markets argue that the effect of the pension funds' accumulation has reduced the mobility of capital and greatly reduced the ability of new-entry firms and growing firms to acquire risk capital.

The last fright thrown into the capital markets was the Meidner plan (named for Rudolph Meidner, chief economist of the Swedish Labor Organization). The essence of the plan was that 20 percent of the pretax profits of all corporations was to be capitalized and given to the workers. That is, new shares were to be issued for these amounts; the shares would be held in trust by the industry's labor union. In due time, the majority of voting shares would be held by the union, and all the firms in the industry would belong to its workers. This stage would be the equivalent of the form of socialism known as syndicalism.

The operational aspects of syndicalism raises some provocative questions. There would be no intraindustry competition; how would the final-product prices be set? Although the workers would own each industry, interindustry differences and conflicts of interests would remain (e. g. , the raw-material industry is likely to have a different notion of a fair price than the processing industry); how would these conflicts be harmonized? Lastly, how would the succession of income rights from the ownership of the industry be settled? Would new workers get the same profit-income share as old workers? What would be the rights of retired workers? How would wages be set between the workers qua workers, and the workers in the roles of owners, directors, and managers?

At any rate, the Meidner plan was dropped from the Socialist party platform before the 1976 election. There is no doubt, however, that the unpopularity of the plan was a contributing factor to the party's defeat in that election.

POSTRECESSION POLICIES

The Swedish economy's real output declined over the 1974-77 period (see Figure 4. 4). Many economic problems, which had been slowly developing, surfaced in the 1974 recession. The extent of the downturn was blinked off by the device of subsidizing production for stock, by subsidizing firms to pay the wages and the retraining costs of redundant workers, and subsidizing the employment of new entrants to the labor force. These devices maintained an artificial level of employment. The officially reported unemployment rate in

FIGURE 4. 4

Industrial Production

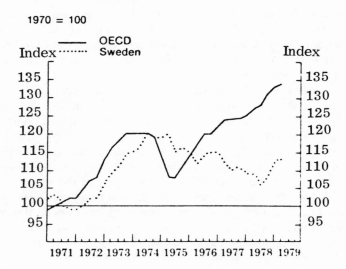

1970 = 100

Source: Erik Lundberg, "Stabilization Policy, Inflation and Profits, "Contemporary Problems of Balance in the Swedish Economy," Skandinaviska Enskilda Banken Quarterly Review, February-March 1979.

1977 was 2. 2 percent; however, it is estimated that if the concealed unemployment of subsidized workers were counted, and partial employment were counted as partial unemployment, the true level of unemployment would have run closer to 11 percent.

In spite of the evident decline in the demand for Swedish products and the pressure of unemployment, the worldwide inflation of prices incited Swedish labor to press for offsetting wage increases. The unions negotiated a 21 percent rise in hourly compensation (in kronor) in 1975, 19 percent in 1976, and 12. 5 percent in 1977. The rise in labor costs (coupled with the krona's appreciation through its link to the Deutsche mark) reduced the competitiveness of Swedish exports. The policies used to maintain employment and domestic income (especially the subsidization of production for stock) in the face of falling foreign demand resulted in appalling deficits in the balance of payments. In effect, this means that the high domestic living standards were being subsidized by foreign loans (or by the sale of Swedish assets held abroad).

To bring the nominal economic relations closer in line with economic reality, the new center government devalued the krona, cut the subsidy for inventory accumulation, and tried to hold the line on money-supply growth and on the increase in wages. In 1977, the krona was devalued by about 15 percent against the major Western European currencies. This should lower the relative international price of Swedish export goods and increase their sale. On the other hand, a devaluation raises the price of imported goods, and also the domestic price of such goods that have a relatively elastic export market and a relatively inelastic supply. * Thus since the devaluation raises the domestic price level, its salutary effects on the country's international accounts will only operate if the factors of production accept a drop in their real income.

If the various income claimants obtain salary and wage increases sufficient to compensate for the full rise in prices, there will be little fall in relative export prices, little decrease in imports, and little improvement in net exports. In such a case, the balance of payments will only improve if a certain amount of unemployment is allowed to

---

*Economists have generally noted that a devaluation raises import prices; they have not always recognized that it raises the domestic price of goods that have both an export and a home market. To take a polar case, suppose a commodity, wheat, selling at $3.00 a bushel, both domestically and internationally, and an exchange rate of 3 marks to the dollar (33 1/3 cents a mark), so that the mark price is 9 marks a bushel. Now, the dollar devalues to 2 marks to $1.00 (50 cents a mark). Assume the foreign demand to be elastic, so that the price of wheat in marks remains at 9 marks, or $4.50, even though the American suppliers now increase their shipments abroad to obtain the more favorable foreign price. Presumably in this case, all wheat would be exported until the domestic price also reached the equilibrium of $4.50. Of course, this example is rather simplistic; the mark price of wheat will fall given the relative increase in American supply. (There is also the possibility that the rise in price will encourage a higher future output; this, too, would discourage a full rise in the current price.) Nevertheless, in any case, the current domestic price would settle at somewhere between the original $3.00 and the new mark price of $4.50 a bushel.

develop. This could be accomplished if the authorities refuse to engage in expansionary monetary or fiscal policy—that is, by refusing to increase the money supply and thus validating the new wage level. This would be, no doubt, a difficult and, at least temporarily, an unpopular course, although it could work, in time, if the unions learned to adjust their expectations.

As such things go, the Swedish policy was relatively brave. The subsidy for production for stock was cut out early in 1977. The money-supply growth was tightened even before the 1976 election. There was an increase in the value-added tax, of 3 percent, and a small personal-income tax cut in 1977 (which, however, was offset by the increase in local taxes). Nevertheless, the central government deficit still remained at 4 percent of the GDP in 1975, 2 percent in 1976, 5 percent in 1977, and is estimated at 8 percent for 1978.

One part of the government's program resembles what the British, in the 1920s, called rationalization of industry. Industries are encouraged to combine in cartels to reduce destructive competition and to concentrate employment in the more efficient firms. This policy might make economic sense if there were a shortage of labor, and the rationalization policy succeeded in directing scarce labor into more productive occupations. (However would not the market accomplish this by adjusting relative wages until the workers, in any case, were employed in the more efficient firms?) Rationalization in England ended up with a part of the labor force on the dole or, in some cases, sharing employment on the job by working reduced hours. (If two workers both work half time, an optimist might say they are sharing employment; a cynic would say that they share the unemployment.)

As part of the program of restructuring the economy, the Swedish government is helping ease the closing of certain plants in shipbuilding and steel. In addition, the government is advancing capital to firms which are assumed to have growth potentials—such as those in the electronics and the engineering industries. Many Swedish financial economists lay the blame for the necessity of making these advances on the lack of fluidity in the capital market. If there were a properly functioning capital market, the growth companies could obtain funds by floating shares or debt issues to private investors or to various competing investment funds. But the fluidity of the financial markets has dried up as the government-sponsored pension funds have come to dominate the market since 1963.

Nevertheless, in spite of all the rigidities in the Swedish structure, perhaps the Swedes will recover from the present economic malaise. If this comes about, it will be due to the greater sense of reality in Swedish labor, and to the residue of pragmatic economic understanding in the older union leadership. (There is, of course, a left-wing section in the union leadership who will resist any recovery program involving worker sacrifices.) Swedish economists hoped to keep the cost on the wage settlement below the rate of inflation for 1979. This would obviously reduce the real wage, but it would also restore the competitiveness of Swedish exports and the profitability of Swedish industry. In actuality, the contracted settlement for 1978 was 6. 3 percent (wage drift and other adjustments brought the actual cost to 9. 3 percent). For 1979, the wage settlement was 5 percent (although the wage drift and extra holidays brought the cost up to 7. 5 percent).[16] Since the price level rose about 10 percent in 1978 and was forecasted to rise about 8 percent for 1979, these settlements would result in a small reduction in real wages. Whether this will be sufficient to bring the economy to a position of actual full employment remains to be seen. In England, on the other hand, as of this writing, workers were demanding romantic wage increases of 20 percent to 40 percent.

OUTLOOK

At present, the Swedes have reached a turning point in their economic development. One option is to try to continue on the path of the last ten years; this would necessitate adjusting to a slow- or a no-growth economy, and at the same time, carrying on a policy of massive income redistribution, implemented by high marginal and average tax rates on all incomes derived from current effort and private investment. The difficulties of this path will become even more apparent in the next few years as the inverted pyramid for the age profile of Swedes effectively increases the burden of the real income transfers required for the payment of retirement pensions and age-related medical costs. Moreover, the social-economic framework will hold only if each economic group eschews the practice of playing for leapfrog gains that may be temporarily covered by money-supply inflation. * Furthermore, income redistribution is more easily accomplished during periods of growth. The path of the slow-growth, redistributional economy is beset with many tensions.

-----

*In a country such as Sweden or the United Kingdom (or the United States), when a money-supply increase is used to support such demands, the policy is accompanied by a negative balance of payments. The positive-balance countries may not wish to finance this kind of behavior indefinitely.

Whether it can be successfully pursued within the framework of a democratic society is open to question.

The other policy alternative involves moving away from some of the programs of welfare subsidies and income redistribution. Indirect taxes on commodities would replace some of the direct taxes on incomes. A reform policy would move toward the employment of user charges to finance the output of some merit goods, reduce the progressivity of the tax system, and turn many of the present governmental services (e. g. , nursery schools) over to private ownership. The idea would be to try to increase profits on investment and increase the return for extra effort, and thus improve labor incentives and the rate of capital formation. Nevertheless, even a better rate of capital formation may not restore the past historic rates of growth. Third-world population-growth pressures, governmental instabilities, and the related supply uncertainties are likely to create problems for the advanced economies, for some time to come. * But this is all the more reason for moving to a more rational and efficient use of resources. For in the present situation, capital formation and productivity are likely to be needed not for the generation of growth, but merely to maintain the present level of living.

---

*As a humanist, one might blink away the rise in oil or copper prices if one could see some concrete improvements in third-world material and political conditions. One does not need to be very cynical to note that most of the potential economic gains are dissipated in military adventuresomeness and unrestrained population growth.

NOTES

1. J. Schumpeter, Capitalism, Socialism, and Democracy, 2d ed. (New York: Harper and Bros. , 1947), p. 325.

2. C. F. Pratten, A Comparison of the Performance of Swedish and United Kingdom Companies (Cambridge: Cambride University Press, 1976), pp. 55–58, 126.

3. World Bank, World Development Report, 1978 (Washington, D. C. : World Bank, August 1978).

4. From my correspondence with Jan Broms, Swedish Federation of Industry, November, 1978.

5. See Yang's comparisons of per-capita real GDP, in Table 1. 2.

6. For a parallel argument, see Samuel Brittan and Peter Lilley, The Delusions of Incomes Policy (London: Temple Smith, 1976), p. 136.

7. Skandinaviska Enskilda Bankens Quarterly Review, no. 1, 1976.

8. See the argument of T. Geiger and Francis Geiger, in Welfare and Efficiency (Washington, D. C. : National Planning Association, 1978), p. 32.

9. Ibid. , p. 33.

10. From my conversation with A. Katsenelinboigen, University of Pennsylvania, February 13, 1979.

11. Geiger and Geiger, op. cit. , p. 29.

12. G. Myrdal, "Time for a Better Tax System," Journal of Economic Debate (Stockholm), no. 7, 1978.

13. A. W. Phillips, "The Relation Between Unemployment and the Rate of Change of Money Wage Rates in the United Kingdom, 1861–1957," Economica, November 1958.

14. See M. Friedman, "The Role of Monetary Policy," American Economic Review, March 1968.

15. See H. P. Minsky, John Maynard Keynes (New York: Columbia University Press, 1975), and Burton G. Malkiel, "Presidential Address," Journal of Finance, Proceedings issue, May 1979.

16. From a letter from Broms, November 1978.

5

INHERENT CONTRADICTIONS

Both the British and Swedish economies have had difficulties in reconciling various goals of economic policy—the British running into various economic frictions early on, and the Swedes, rather more recently. In neither country is the situation catastrophic; nevertheless, a sense of social and political uneasiness has begun to permeate these societies. There is a feeling that certain trends will need to be diverted, some operating beliefs amended, and some of the economic structure reshaped if the economies are to recover their vitality. It is clear that the savants of soft Marxism and the students of the tomes of social democracy do not possess the answers to all questions.

There are some conflicts and problems, underlying all organized societies, for which socialism does not provide a better solution than does a free market economy, or even as good a solution. This does not deter some socialists from launching general tirades against capitalism, since they are content with assuming the role of critics. However, one may wonder whether a purely critical stance is ever intellectually valid. There is a well-known rule of scientific methodology that a working hypothesis or theory can only be overturned by another theory. Contradictory factual evidence reduces the degree of reliance to be placed on the existing theory; but the old theory cannot be displaced except by the construction of a better hypothesis, one which explains the new phenomena as well as the observation predicted by the established theory. This is a rule of modesty that enforces a certain continuity in the sciences and forces the investigator to present his facts within a rational framework.

It is a pity that a similar rule is not enforced in the discussion of policy and in the discussion of alternative political and economic

systems. * Too often, the critics of capitalism proffer semantic ob-
scurities, aphorisms, and double-entendre mottoes when asked for
specific programs. (For example, such mottoes as "production for
use and not for profit" sound deliberately obscure to a trained economist. It must mean that a commissar or committee will decide what
is to be produced, instead of industry producing the articles that
people are willing to buy at a price that covers cost.) When asked to
explain how some specific problems or flaws in the market economy
would be handled in an alternate system, the critics of the market
system may tell you that it is sufficient that they be critics. They
will consider it a hostile question if asked to describe the actual
operational results of an existing socialist system, in contrast to
those of capitalism. Nevertheless, when a one-sided, purely critical
attitude permeates intellectual discourse, it clouds the ability to
weight reasonable policy alternatives. It is, of course, an abhorrent
development to the social democrats, but one might note that on the
wilder boundary of events in our time, where politics degenerates
into tragic violence, the unwillingness to provide alternative exem-
plary models is a pronounced characteristic of such anarchistic revo-
lutionary groups as the Weathermen or the Red Brigades. The professed sole goal of these groups is the overturning of the present
order, since whatever follows must of necessity be better.

My mother used to say of certain people: "He loves mankind,
but he dislikes people." Someone who loves mankind too much may
be incapable of accepting imperfect people in a less-than-perfect
society. In the general context of dealing with policy, especially
social policy, an English aphorism expresses a parallel thought:
"Perfection is the enemy of the good."

Of course, there is a role for economic and social tinkerers.
Their function is to point out the obvious gaps in the provision of
social goods and to devise economic safety nets for those who, out

---

*In his latest book, Beyond Boom and Crash, Robert Heilbroner
points to the recent strains in the poorly directed capitalist economies, including the United States, Sweden, and Great Britain. But,
who has well-directed economies (Czechoslovakia, Bulgaria, the
USSR?), we are not told. Heilbroner makes the alienation of the
assembly-line worker equivalent to Marxism's increasing impover-
ishment of labor. Heilbroner points to the Volvo plant in Sweden as
a company which has experimented with methods to relieve the mo-
notony of factory works. (He might have noted the recent production
and financial problems of Volvo.)[1]

of inability to provide for themselves, would otherwise crash. The
metaphor is easily susceptible to change, however. In the weavings
of ever-better devices, the safety nets may imperceptibly become
gill nets, strangling the creatures moving upstream.

At any rate, the workings of the British and Swedish economies
reveal some innate contradictions and frictions of socialistically oriented societies. The roots of these contradictions lie in the unavoid-
able conflicts of certain values. These conflicts are not, as Marxists
are fond of arguing, simply the peculiar aberrations of a market
economy, which would automatically disappear in a socialist society.

THE INHERENT CONTRADICTIONS OF CAPITALISM

The Marxist scientific critique of capitalism rests on the system's inherent contradictions, which, according to the critique, must
lead to its inevitable collapse. To be (perhaps somewhat unfairly)
brief, the capitalist system must continually reinvest its surplus
value (profits) to maintain the income cycle. Surplus value arises
from the use of circulating capital (current assets or stocks of inventory), which is in essence the fund used to employ labor. To make a
profit from employing a share of the labor force, however, one must
have fixed capital (plant and equipment) to which the workers can be
productively attached. This profit (the surplus value which is derived
from the exploitative employment of labor) is normally reinvested in
fixed capital, in a competitive attempt by individual capitalists to
capture their share of the surplus value. However, this deepening of
fixed capital investment brings about a fall in the overall ratio of
circulating capital to fixed capital, which implies a fall in the rate
of surplus value earned on fixed capital—i.e., a decline in the rate
of profit.

At this point, with the fall in profit, the system experiences an
inevitable crisis. The economy suffers from overinvestment; since
there is insufficient profit incentive, the surplus value is no longer
spent on new capital; the result is a falloff in total activity, increased
unemployment, and economic depression. The depression will last
until the excess capital is worked off over time or destroyed in a
capitalist-plotted war, after which a new boom can commence. In
time, as the system becomes more wealthy, the crises will become
deeper and will appear closer together, until all collapses.

A necessary feature of the model is the assumption that wages
are held down to subsistence levels by the iron law of wages or the
reserve army of the unemployed; otherwise, a critic could argue that
a secular rise in consumption spending could help to maintain aggre-

gate income and full employment, dampening the need for continuous increases in the ratio of investment.

At any rate, at the base of the classic Marxist critique of the capitalist system is this inherent contradiction: that as the economy becomes progressively more wealthy, it becomes unable to even provide steady employment to its impoverished workers.

This is powerful stuff. It has captured the minds of many people because it skirts close to the truth. But the complexities of reality and the diversity of economic structures belie the sweeping model. Reasonable monetary and fiscal policies can keep an economy close to full employment. There has been no persistent shortage of aggregate demand in the post-World War II period. And it would be difficult for any statistician to find evidence to prove the growing immiserization of labor in any capitalist economy over the last 200 years.

Moreover, the notion that full employment is maintained without difficulty in a command Marxist economy falls under some doubt. These economies create a sufficiency of aggregate demand, but since the aggregate supply or production function is either tight or structurally imbalanced, the economy is generally left with a surplus of purchasing power. Popular goods are often scarce, price controlled, and rationed. The excess money stock finds its way into a myriad of illegal, semilegal, and semiofficial black and grey markets. The continuous repressed inflation leads to illegal tipping, the purchase of special personal privileges, and a variety of minor corruptive practices.

EXTERNAL EXPLOITATION

Recently, because the fact is that the market systems have operated as well as, or better than the socialized economies, the more subtle Marxists have tended to shift their attack from the internal workings of the capitalist system to its external relations. The key words are racism and imperialism. The role of the domestic proletariat as the victim of exploitation has been replaced by the case of the third-world nations. There is hardly room here for a full-fleshed rebuttal of this new scenario. Suffice it to say that most of the countries of the Southern Hemisphere have experienced considerable growth in gross national incomes in the postwar period. In almost every case, however, the increase in per-capita income has been disappointingly low because of the high rate of population growth. It is difficult to believe that this proclivity to increase the number of people should be properly laid to the fault of racism, imperialism, or capitalism. In much of the third world, almost all plans of rational economic development have been defeated by unreasonable rates of population growth. It would be useful if some idealistic energies could be diverted from shooting up the system and directed instead toward ameliorating this rather real and immediate problem.

Although the sweeping Marixist critique does not provide much insight as to how cures for social ills would be actually effected, and even if actual Marxist societies are not that appealing in operation, one cannot deny the existence of specific problems that arise in the market economy and require rational attention. Nevertheless, since many of these problems appear to be inherent in the nature of any society, one can only hope to devise remedies that will ameliorate the situation, reduce the occurrence of the problem in the future, and try to avoid side effects that may be worse than the original condition. To employ violence in an attempt to achieve a utopian cure is to be in the grip of a wicked and blood-wasting delusion.

INCOME DISTRIBUTION

The most obvious and felt inequity in the market system is the disparity in the distribution of incomes. According to neoclassical theory, each productive factor will be paid the value of its marginal product. Roughly, the incomes of the various classes of productive inputs, natural resources, labor, and accumulated capital are determined by their relative productivity. It also follows that various classes of labor and individuals in various professions are largely rewarded according to the value of their skills and talents: people endowed with highly desired, unique (not easily duplicable) skills and talents may receive very high incomes. Such incomes may lead to invidious comparisons and cause jealousy and unhappiness among some observers. However, a more reasonable cause for uneasiness in contemplating the possibility of a purely market-determined distribution of income lies at the other end of the spectrum. What would be the fate of the weak and the helpless in a pure market system?

The pure market economists have elicited criticism by seemingly ignoring the problem of the truly helpless; it might appear that in an absolute market system, they would be left to starve. But of course, economics is a social science, and it would be a rare economic model that contemplated the distribution of product taking place outside an implicit nexus of social units (families or tribes) and institutions of social traditions and obligations. These social institutions perform the function of providing sustenance to those without their own means. Nevertheless, pure technical economics, with its basis of rationality, cannot explain the derivation of and the existence of various familial, charitable, and merciful institutions.

These stem from values and instincts that are not in the purview of more circumscribed economic analysis. Nevertheless, it is clear that in any viable society, the felt necessity arises for some exogenous basis of shared values that sanctions certain behaviors and proscribes others (and it may be this basis of shared values that sometimes seems tragically lacking in our modern societies). [2]

The basic primitive social unit for allocating consumption is the family. Goods are allocated within the family on some basis other than productivity; otherwise, the children would starve. This may seem so obvious as to be taken for granted. However, one notion of some social reformers is that the family is a repressive social form that should be amended or abolished. Still, it is beginning to become clear that the economic costs thrust on the rest of society, when family responsibilities become easily abandoned, are really quite high.

In a civilized society, the bonds of responsibility will extend outside the family. The maimed, the retarded, and the incompetent are not left to starve, although their productive capacity might be very low. In earlier societies, when family support was not available, these people were taken care of by various charities. So even in a market society, there was always some form of income redistribution and some leveling of incomes.

The modern welfare society supplements the private charities; it finances aid through taxes (rather than through voluntary contribution), and to the list of traditional clients—the sick, the aged, abandoned children—it adds those thrown into difficult times by natural disasters or economic dislocations. As exemplified by the English and Swedish economies, it becomes apparent that when the clientele is continually multiplied and the administrative and personnel costs are counted in, the provision of various types of aid can become a large part of the GNP. At a certain point, the costs of providing welfare aid and social subsidies can begin to fall heavily not only on the high- but on the average-income recipient.

The warnings of conservatives early in this century, that too much income redistribution could reduce incentives and efficiency, were probably premature. Because these warnings could be safely ignored at the time, they probably had a perverse political effect. The problems of efficiency have only become evident as the various social programs have deepened and widened. It is perhaps only now becoming apparent that a combination of very heavy marginal taxes and publicly provided social services can reduce the tradeoff between effort and income (i. e. , lower the incentive to work at the margin) and attenuate the ties of family responsibility. Nevertheless, the dilemma is not peculiarly a capitalist or socialist problem. It would surface with the same force in a Marxist society.

The conceptual gap between the willingness to provide a minimal income floor and the notion that true social justice requires absolutely equal incomes is fairly wide, but not impossible to leap over. [3] In practice, however, one finds absolute equality advocated mainly by middle-class people who, observing their rich friends, do not realize that they themselves are in the minority higher-income brackets. Moreover, the concept of justice through income equality receives a cool reception when one suggests that income redistribution might not stop at national borders, but could include Bangladesh, Bolivia, and India. (When put this way, the equal-income notion is not received with much warmth from Eastern European economists, either.) Moreover, even on an ideal level, equal income is not everyone's idea of fairness. Even if the qualities which lead to a higher income might be inherent or innate, a gift rather than something acquired, the more hard-working, talented, or skilled people seem to desire some monetary recognition over their less talented counterparts, and can become unhappy if it is not forthcoming. Further, the question of just how equal incomes should be is not solved by the theory of the Marxist scripture, nor by Marxist societies in practice. *

POPULATION PROBLEMS

There are any number of other problems which are presumed to be inherent in a capitalist economy, but which, on closer observation, show up just as readily in a socialist economy. The problem of excess population growth relative to resources was not even broached by Marx, since he felt that the concept of declining returns was a fiction invented by the bourgeois economists to explain rents and poverty. The early Mao Tse-tung ignored the population problem entirely. It was solved by the aphorism, "Every person is born with two hands and but one mouth." Of course, this simplistic approach was eventually abandoned.

The factors that might make for a reasonable population growth are not fully understood. The security furnished by old-age pensions, family responsibility for adequate child care, and a desire to achieve

---

*"From each according to his ability, to each according to his needs": the Marxist aphorism is beautiful. Unfortunately, neither ability nor need is an easily definable quantum. The seeds of tyranny are clearly discernible when in the end, some outside supervisor defines and demands a person's ability to produce and decides on the person's needs.

and maintain certain educational levels may all be relevant factors. The type of economic structure is not too important. China, India, Iran, Egypt, Turkey, Mexico, Venezuela, and the Arab countries all have population problems. Japan has dampened the population growth that prevailed before World War II. In some countries, the growth situation is reversed, and demographers and pension economists worry about the consequences of an inverted population/age distribution (e. g. , in Sweden); in the Soviet Union, there is some concern over the decline in the population of Great Russians relative to other peoples in the USSR. The list of countries that have population problems is apparently not correlated to their pronounced economic philosophy.

CONSUMPTION VERSUS CAPITAL INVESTMENT

The question of how much to provide in present consumer goods, and how much to invest in capital, is a persistent problem in a mixed economy. Within the theory of the market economy, the division between current consumption and capital formation is solved automatically. The individual's willingness to abstain from present consumption (i. e. , to save) is rewarded by the interest rate, so that the saver obtains the promise of being able to enjoy greater consumption in the future. The level of the interest rate at the margin determines the supply of savings. The demand for saved resources to be used for capital formation (i. e. , buildings, factories, inventories, tools, machinery, and ships) is determined by the marginal productivity of capital. In a given economy with a given income distribution, the intersection of the supply-of-savings function and the marginal-productivity-of-capital function determines the interest rate (or the cost of capital). Thus out of a given gross output, the interest rate determines the amount spent for current consumption and the amount saved and placed in new capital formation. The output of new capital helps determine the potential increase in output in the future, i. e. , the rate of economic growth.

Most modern economies have intervened in this process to a greater or lesser extent. A great deal of capital formation is socially determined, and takes the form of physical investment in the governmental or nonmarket sector, or is turned into human capital by subsidized investment in training, education, or health.

Nevertheless, even on a theoretical level, the Marxist framework contains no formulations for splitting the output between consumer and producer goods. Since a market-derived interest rate is anathema to the Marxists, they have no objective guideline to determine the tradeoff between the sacrifice of present consumption and the production of more goods later. In practice, in the command economies, the balance between the present and the future is struck by some planning committee. (To be fair, some notion of an interest rate or present value has by necessity crept into the Marxist analysis, if only as a rationing device to decide between different projects.) That the decision of the planners is not always acceptable is attested to by food riots and endemic complaints over the shortage of consumer goods.

The mixed economies such as Sweden and England have allowed considerable leeway for the functioning of private financial markets. Nevertheless, in England and increasingly in Sweden, socialist planners have intervened, to what many consider a harmful extent, in the capital markets. As early as Roy Harrod's pamphlet of 1947, "Are These Hardships Necessary?", we find a criticism that capital was wasted because of the failure to observe business principles. The term "business principles" refers to the criterion that an investment project should be expected to cover the normal return on capital—that is, the interest rate plus a sufficient cover for risk.

However, in any economy, private, mixed, or socialist, the decision as to the amount to be invested in social capital must be made outside the market system. Social capital is used to produce public goods; public goods are best defined as those goods which have interrelated utilities, or those where the total social benefits exceed each individual's count of capturable private benefits, so that, left to the price system, the private demand for the goods would be below the optimum social demand. For example, a clear case for classification as a public good might be made for a basic level of education available to all citizens, because capital productivity increases with a trained labor force, and because almost all people have their welfare (i.e., personal utility) raised by living in a reasonably literate society.

The theoretical decision on the optimum level of social investment is the same as that for private investment; at the margin, the stream of forecasted future social benefits, discounted at the rate of the cost of capital to society, should equal the additional amount of investment. It is difficult, of course, to estimate the flow of benefits. The level of benefits may legitimately be evaluated at different levels by different-minded people; however, the problem of making rational decisions is made even more difficult when socialist economists such as S. A. Marglin further obfuscate the issue by proposing the use of a social cost of capital or discount rate, which is even below the government's borrowing rate on the market. It is clear that on the contrary, the cost of capital employed to evaluate government projects should at least be equal to the weighted average private cost of capital at the margin. [4]

THE ABUSE OF COMMON RESOURCES

Pollution and the overexploitation of common natural resources, such as overfishing, are often blamed on the greediness of the capitalist system. There is no stricture, however, in the Marxist literature which would prevent the extermination of species, or the pollution of water and air, or the congestion of traffic, and the accumulation of dirt on city streets. These phenomena are all aspects of the same underlying factor, the existence of a common property resource. Common property resources are overexploited because there is no price charged for their use. The costs of using them are only partially reflected in the calculations of the user, and the extra social costs are distributed over a wide segment of society. Simply put, a householder may allow the smoke of his furnace to be floated off in the wind as the cheapest method of disposal. His costs as an individual may be quite low, but the overall costs to the community—when a sufficient population density is reached—may be quite high in terms of health hazards and increased laundry expenses. Another example of a miscalculation of external costs is overfishing, where the maximum present value of all present and future catches would call for a lower degree of fishing effort, allowing for an optimum level of sustainable fish population, but the individual fishing boat does not count in its decisions the rising costs of a declining stock for all the fishermen. In economics, these general phenomena are called external diseconomies. When ignored, they lead to lower overall allocative efficiency and lower total welfare.

The problems of pollution and overexploitation of the environment are just as endemic in Russia as they are in the market economies; the problems are not confined to capitalist economies. The disputes between the Soviet production managers and the environmentalists arise because the production manager is rewarded for his measurable output, and he is not charged for the use or the degradation of the environment. [5] Of course, there is general agreement that since the end of World War II, Great Britain has made great strides in reducing the degree of surface-water pollution and in improving the quality of the air. (However, it is hard to see that this is due in any unique way to the socialist economy.)

The problem of external diseconomies arises from the use of a common resource—where there is no defined ownership right. It can be solved by internalizing the external costs; that is, by making these costs overt to the users of the resource. This can be done, for example, by charging a fee, establishing private property rights to the resource, or by the imposition of external sanctions—legal penalties and controls on the use of the resource. None of these remedies is easier to implement in the socialist scheme of things than in the

private economy; moreover, one solution, turning the common resource into individual property holdings, is improbable in a socialist
milieu.

Nuclear Power and Socialism

It is common, among the critics of nuclear power, to place the
blame for the construction of nuclear power-generating plants on the
greed and the exploitative nature of the privately owned electric utilities. Yet it is an incontrovertible fact that whereas in 1978, 12.5
percent of U.S. electricity output came from nuclear plants, the
comparable figure was 14 percent in the United Kingdom one year
earlier, in 1977 (it was 11.2 percent in 1975 and 13.1 percent in
1976). The nuclear electric output in Sweden was the highest in the
Western world, 25 percent of total electricity sources in 1978 (up
from 14.9 percent in 1975, 18.5 percent in 1976, and 22.1 percent
in 1977).[6] The point is simply that these socialist countries, with
publicly owned generating systems, derive a larger percentage of
their electric energy from nuclear plants than does the United States.
(The accusation that the capitalist system is at fault for sheltering
this industry is simply another illustration of the old adage that "any
stick will do to beat the dog.")
Apparently in England, most major groups in society have
come to an acceptance of the nuclear power industry. However, in
Sweden, peculiarly enough, it is the Social Democrats who have
accepted the nuclear power industry (along with, to be fair, the
Liberals and the Conservatives); the Center Party (essentially a
small-holders group) is strongly opposed and is pledged to phase it
out.
Now, it does seem to me that the advantages of nuclear power
probably outweigh its possible dangers. But the main point in the
present context is that the decision on the use of nuclear power has
nothing at all to do with the dispute between capitalism and socialism.

X-EFFICIENCY AND THE ENTREPRENEUR

Whereas there are many problems which are common to both
socialist and capitalist economies, there are some functions performed in the free-enterprise economy that are perforce neglected
under socialism. One such function is entrepreneurship in the sense
of implementing innovation—forcing new products and new methods
of production and distribution into the economy. The socialist
authority is probably not very appreciative of that type of entrepre-

neurship which engages in arbitraging in a broad sense, by moving commodities from one area to another, or in speculative entrepreneurship that may move commodities from one time period to the next, by holding inventories or speculating in futures. No doubt, the socialists might approve an innovator who takes a superior method of production from one area where it is known, and introduces it to another, but not if he does it for a substantial private reward.

Nevertheless, the function of the entrepreneur in seizing upon the opportunities that develop in an open society—in a sense, arbitraging away inefficiencies, thus bringing the economy to a higher state of X-efficiency—plays an important role in the rate of economic development. The entrepreneur's role in introducing innovations of all sorts is, of course, central to Schumpeter's vision of economic dynamics, and is exposited in a more theoretical manner by Harvey Leibenstein.[7] Although managers who are efficient enough for more-or-less routine operations in the nationalized industries may be readily available, the supply of true innovators may be constricted in a socialist state.

In addition to the loss of innovation, Leibenstein argues that publicly owned industries on the whole become less efficient over time than privately owned industries because the uneconomic or the poorly directed firms are not allowed to fail. Moreover, in the socialized industries, humdrum management is rewarded—it is less risky; in a socialist economy the punishment for the failed risk taker is disproportionately large compared to the payoff for success.

International Trade

The question of setting prices and terms of trade for international commerce is a difficult one for fully socialized economies. Often some sort of barter arrangement is made; often the less powerful country thinks it may have been taken advantage of. Although it is embarrassing, in actual practice, the reference points for Marxist trade are often the relative prices that have been set in the capitalist markets. This means that trade between Marxist countries would become more difficult if commercial markets no longer existed. This point might be elaborated on; however, to be frank, the growth of nationalized trade policies and controlled cartels and monopolies in the trading world takes some of the force out of the argument.

The Performing Arts

The provision of arts and music is a difficult task in a market economy, because these outputs often appeal to highly trained minority tastes. On the other hand, the supply of artists willing and desiring to try out their creative talents, and to obtain some recognition from patrons and critics, is high relative to the effective demand. This means that the way of the artist, poet, or musician is hard, especially for the young and unrecognized. The socialist countries do seem to consider the arts as a merit or public goal, deserving of some treasury support. This has influenced some of the intelligentsia toward a more favorable attitude toward socialism—as a kind of culture where their tastes might be more influential. Of course, on the other side of the coin, is the fear that a sole reliance on government support, without any competitive element, could lead to a loss of creativity and result in a stultifying conformity. (Conformity need not necessarily be the result of government intervention. It can just as well arise from the tyranny of intellectual fashion as it affects foundation grant committees.) Nevertheless, the question of how far, and under what system of government grants, foundation gifts, private contributions, and admission fees, one might wish to support the arts is common to all the mixed economies.

BURDENING THE BOURGEOISIE

The democratic socialists are an exasperating lot. One suspects that they have good motives. * However, their unwillingness to settle for reasonable results in such matters as income distribution or the amelioration of poverty leads, in practice, to a piling up of regulations and government rules, to such an extent that negative results emerge. The supply curve of effort turns away from productive labor and toward a form of game playing. Depending on the situation or on personal proclivities, a large portion of economic energy is spent on conforming to the rules or on bending or dodging them.

The main thrust of socialist policy is directed toward making incomes more equal. The rewards that go to special talents, skills, intelligence, training, application, and luck are to be relatively reduced. (It can be agreed that the reward for luck is a form of economic rent—and as such, could be justifiably taxed away. The problem is that the sources of high incomes are often intermingled and

---

*I have to enter one personal comment here. The anti-American prejudices of some left-wing European intellectuals can become annoying. The responsibility for almost everything that goes wrong in the world is placed on the American. On the other hand, the Soviets' more-egregious actions are somehow excused and rationalized away. Yet it is clear that the last place in the world these people would choose to live is the Soviet Union.

hard to distinguish, so that a tax on luck might turn out to be a tax
on skill and application.)

At any rate, a relatively high tax on the incremental incomes
of people with outstanding performing, musical, or artistic talent,
or on the income of research scientists, probably does not have too
deleterious an effect on their total output. These people are anxious
to find an outlet for their talents and may not be too concerned about
the return for their efforts at the margin. (The fact that artists,
scholars, and scientists might be content with a relatively modest
reward does not preclude some of them, individually, from receiving
high incomes in a market economy; various institutions bidding for
the output of rare talent or genius can bring the price up quite high.
The socialist economies must come reasonably close to meeting the
world price for desirable skills, or suffer a brain drain.) However,
for the mechanic with good skills, the applied professions, good
managers and administrators, the mere opportunity to exercise
talent and skill may not be a sufficient reward. These are not glamor-
ous jobs; the administrator's accomplishments are not always apparent to the public. The manager has to be intelligent, meticulous, and
careful to observe deviations from the norm, but much of his work
is routine. Apparently, it is in these areas of activity that a high
marginal tax rate begins to have a dampening effect on effort. If one
is not to be given any special reward, there are many jobs more
appealing than being a manager. The incentives to develop middle-
and higher-level skills and to exercise caring managerial attitudes
may be vitiated by socialist antielitism.

If the socialists are unsympathetic to the idea of allowing an
extra return for middle-level skills, they are even more disdainful
of the justifications for a return on property or capital. Under democratic socialism in normal times, because capital will find ways to
be productive, the effect of this attitude is not too noticeable. But
there are exogenous factors, circumstances external to the economy,
which can lower the real wealth or income of a given country. These
might be natural circumstances, such as floods, droughts, bad crops,
or the disappearance of the school of anchovies off the Peruvian
coast, or man-made disasters, such as riots in the copper mines,
strikes in the coal fields, or the creation of illegal crude oil cartels. *

---

*I use the word "illegal" advisedly. An obvious conspiracy to
control output, and thus price, would not be legal under either common or Roman law. Moreover, the initial breach of contract and the
expropriation of the private owners of the oil fields were hardly
models of legal procedures. (Of course, it is my contention that oil

The effect of such developments is to increase the scarcity of raw-material resources or to lower the terms of trade (i. e. , the cost of imported goods rises relative to the prices obtainable for export goods). When due to negative developments, the amount of available resources declines, or the terms of trade move in an unfavorable direction, the overall real income of the affected country or region must fall. *

In a reasonably competitive and flexible economy, this fall in income will be diffused throughout the economy; real wages will fall, and so will the total of income derived from property. (This will cause a writedown of the real value of the existing stock of property or capital assets.) However, the rate of return on new capital need not fall. If the rate of return on net increments of capital is sustained, there should be a continuing investment of capital; and in the normal course of events, in a relatively short period, the previously prevailing real income level should be restored.

But suppose economic policy is dominated by the view that the poor and/or the working class must in no way suffer because of untoward external events. In this case, it is not too difficult to design a set of policies, such that in the short run, the cost of the downturn falls mainly on capital. (I am loathe to lay out the specifics of such policies for fear they will encourage harmful emulation. However, I suppose a careful reader will already have found most of the recipes in the previous chapters.) For example, one could raise the minimal wage, and bargain for a higher nominal wage to try to hold the real wage constant; one would then attempt to offset the resulting rise in unemployment by increasing the money supply. Income policies, price controls, rationing, and defining profits, for tax purposes, as the revenue in excess of historic costs—all of these may be pretty useful in reducing profits and discouraging capital

---

companies were reasonably competitive. The present cartel was organized only after the various petroleum corporations were summarily deprived of their investments and rights in the oil fields.)

*One must be careful not to abuse analysis based on movements in the terms of trade. A country may find its export industries lowering price (and increasing sales) because of an improvement in productivity. This may lower the terms of trade, but the actual real income of the country will rise. Latin American economists often blame their countries' problems on (unfair) deteriorations in the terms of trade. More likely, the root causes are unstable political institutions and excess population growth.

formation. Unfortunately, the long-run effect of this set of policies is that all sectors suffer. The rigid real-wage policies raise the natural rate of unemployment. Even if the real wage of those that remain employed is safeguarded, the total real wage bill declines, and if we divide the real wage bill by the total number in the labor force, including the unemployed, average real wages decline. Moreover, because of the lower level of employment and production, property income too will fall. This must be a loss if we consider property-income recipients also as citizens.

Some Keynesians have done economics a great disservice by ignoring the master's contention that the decline in the marginal productivity of labor must reduce the real wage unit on the approach path to full employment. In the original Keynesian analysis, this takes place through a slight rise in prices, while the money wage remains constant. This has been called the money-wage illusion; actually, there is no illusion at all, because the tradeoff for the lower real wage unit is an increase in the total volume of employment and a rise in total real wages and in the GNP.

The point of the foregoing argument is that if the real wage unit must decline on the final push toward full employment, then, reasoning in reverse, a resistance to lowering the real wage unit, in the face of an external economic shock, will lead to an increase in unemployment at the margin. However, the worst aspect of a policy designed to throw the readjustment costs entirely on capital is its deleterious effect on the rate of capital formation. The reduction in the rate of real investment means a stretching out of the time required to repair the losses sustained by the economy.

PROBLEMS OF A SLOW-GROWTH ECONOMY

There is a current train of thought that holds that the advanced economies (capitalist or socialist) have reached an absolute level of wealth that is quite sufficient to satisfy all reasonable needs. [8] Under these conditions, the goal of economic growth is a snare and a delusion and is, in itself, the cause of most of our social and economic uneasiness. * A sensible society would argue for a program of actual retrogression.

---

*A large portion of what the critics consider the evils of growth, such as pollution or crowding, are external economic costs or diseconomies. The solution would be to have the contributors to pollution

A corollary of a no-growth policy frame of mind is that there should be a more equal distribution of income, because in a no-growth economy, there is a lesser need of savings for capital formation and a lesser need of incentives for production and efficiency. * A deliberate no-growth policy leads to a push toward socialism under the covert notion that in order to smother the forces of growth, controls would be useful to dampen initiative and to stifle the drive toward the acquisition of wealth. The picture of an enforced no-growth policy is actually rather dull, if not somewhat unpleasant.

Now it may be that in fact, we are entering a new slow-growth era. This is the result of the relative (artificial or real) shortage of natural resources, and (the other side of the coin) of the growing costs of, and the more explicit accounting for, environmental pollution and degradation, and a resulting desired diversion of capital to the construction of antipollution devices. (Pollution uses natural resources. When there are wide areas of open space, air, and water, the costs of pollution are minimal; these costs rise as the environment becomes more constricted.) Thus, this new slow-growth situation is not a deliberately selected policy path, but the natural outcome of the frictions generated as the growth economies have begun to run up against various external barriers.

In this situation, it is not clear that socialism will function better than the market. For one thing, capital investment is not a redundant factor when resources become tighter. Capital is a partial substitute for natural resources; that is, such capital investments as land-reclamation projects, aquaculture ponds, desalination plants, plants to recycle junk and scrap, or plants to harness ocean power all require large amounts of investment; but these projects would

---

pay their fair share of these costs; there would be a lower rate of growth of bookkeeping income, but in return, the level of pollution would decrease.

*For economists mainly, it should be noted that a more equal income distribution would lower aggregate savings (increase consumption) only if the cross-sectional consumption function were curvilinear. That is, the marginal propensity to consume would have to fall as we moved to higher-income groups. Although the average propensity to save is obviously higher for higher-income groups, there is no clear-cut evidence that this holds true for the marginal propensity to save. On the other hand, if the cross-sectional marginal propensity to consume is constant, then a redistribution of income will not significantly change the level of aggregate savings and consumption. It may, however, dampen the incentive to invest.

offset a shortage of resources that once might have been obtainable on less expensive terms. When natural resources become scarcer, a large amount of savings and capital investment may be needed not to recapture past rates of growth, but merely to maintain a modest rate of improvement, or perhaps even to hold the economy where it is.

The capital investment would be forthcoming, in a free market economy, as the price of the scarce natural resources (e. g. , petroleum, natural gas, wild fish) rose relative to the capital-intensive substitutes.

Nevertheless, the economic-policy makers must allow for an adequate return on capital if resource-saving investments are to be made and maintained. * One must expect and tolerate a return for innovation and entrepreneurship, since the ability of capital to replace natural resources will depend heavily on individual initiative and reward for the discovery and the adaptation of new resource-saving techniques. All this means that an economy which hopes to adapt to a new set of circumstances may find it difficult to do so if it insists on maintaining rigidity in its income distribution.

LEGISLATING CONTENTMENT

In an otherwise generally favorable review, a book by Raymond Aron, In Defense of Decadent Europe, was criticized by the New York Times book reviewer for its cool common sense. [9] The problem with a reasonably successful bourgeois capitalist economy is that it has no heroic vision. (The same plaint is voiced by Irving Kristol in the last chapter of his book, Two Cheers for Capitalism.)[10] It is indeed true that the rewards of the liberal capitalist society are rather commonplace and tend to be private. The social goals of the system are rather limited because they require some sort of consensus before they can be pursued, and room must be allowed for objectors to go their own way within reason. No wonder that the more romantic dissenters within the system, seeing it has not dissolved all injustices,

---

*In the past, the rate of resource loss was almost imperceptible. Growth in real per-capita income took place as capital formation added to the total of capital plus resources available per worker. In the future, a large part of capital formation may be resource saving, and the total of resources and capital per worker may not grow very rapidly.

would prefer to break it all up and remold it closer to their hearts' desire (if they could only think what that might be).

But, of course, it is unfair to lay the charge of mundaneness solely at the doorstep of capitalism. What are the heroic rewards in a reasonably successful socialist state? It is the march toward socialism, and not its achievement, that enthralls its followers.

The essay by Sigmund Freud, <u>Civilization and Its Discontents</u>, contains the seminal suggestion that some of the conflict between man and his society may be innate and inevitable. [11] Growing up into a functioning citizen involves curbing or sublimating inherent primitive instincts. It involves learning to restrain actions which could be directed to the immediate satisfaction of a primitive drive, but which, in the longer run, would bring the disapproval or retaliation of others. The tradeoff for the sublimation of primitive drives is the cooperation and support given to the individual by the group and its culture. Nevertheless, the conflict between self-sacrifice and the aggressive instincts is never fully resolved, and for different personalities, the conflict leads to varying levels of unhappiness or discontent with the necessary constraints of the culture.

Freud can hardly have meant that there are no objective facts which could cause rational discontent or an acute sense of injustice leading to reasoned action. He was describing a general condition of malaise, for which a direct cause might be missing, and which, nevertheless, could result in a violent and bloody outbreak against the normal codes of social conduct. His prototype would more likely be a fascist (or, in the present world, a member of the Red Brigades) than an intellectual Marxist. Nevertheless, there exists sufficient reason why the orthodox Marxist philosophers of material determinism consider Freud a heretic—a bourgeois apologist at best. For the pristine Marxist philosophy holds that social discontent flows out of objective factors—the inanities and injustices inherent in the capitalist organization of production in a system of private property, and not out of an innate conflict between biological drives and the constraints of a civilized culture.

Freud's sin was to suggest that after all the sacrifices have been made and the full socialist state established, there will still be an irreducible core of unhappiness. Contentment and personal happiness are not purely a matter of economic organization. The problem of how to bring a measure of happiness to people can be dealt with as effectively in a capitalist society as in a socialist one.

REFORMING THE REFORMS

Suppose one wished to move away from the socialist superstructure, such as that erected in the United Kingdom and Sweden (and, to a somewhat lesser degree, in the mixed economies of Western Europe and the United States); in what direction would one proceed? The basic reform would involve some shift from the provision of social income toward allowing more private income and private expenditure. This would restore some of the rewards of labor and help restore the morale of those who elect to be hardworking and relatively sober. Direct taxes (especially the high marginal taxes on income) would be reduced and proportionately more of the government fisc could be collected by indirect taxes. (Some features of this program parallel that of Margaret Thatcher, the British prime minister.) Surely, the separate corporate income tax would be abolished and corporate income imputed and taxed as part of personal income. (A more sweeping reform would abolish the present earnings tax altogether and substitute an Irving Fisher-type tax that would rest on the amount expended on consumption, no matter what the source. Such a tax can have a degree of progression if one wishes; at a minimum, a certain base level of consumption could be exempted from taxation.)

User charges could be implemented to cover the full or partial costs of many services now provided free. This might be especially useful in the area of higher education; by increasing the resources available to the institutes of higher education, it might actually enable them to take in more students. (The British system of higher education is a rationing system. The education is free, but one must have a ticket to get in.) On the provision of health care, one might try a cost-sharing basis where, for example, one-third of the charges are paid by the patient, and the other two-thirds, by a third party or insurer. Catastrophic illnesses could be fully covered by a social insurer. Under this system, one could have private medicine; there would be some competition as doctors would consider the price to be charged versus the resulting number of steady patients.

To make the market system complete, the tuition charges for higher professional training should be at full cost. Every student could finance training costs through a comprehensive loan system. The student would pay interest and amortize the principal out of his future professional earnings, with the payments correlated with his income; and to make the whole transaction fair, both the repayment of the principal and the payment of the current interest should be deductible from the income tax base—since the repayment of the principal would be considered to roughly correspond to the depreciation of the human-capital investment put into the training program. This proposition might be clarified by illustration. Suppose the full cost of medical-education tuition were $15,000 per year. With accumulated interest, at the time he commenced practice, the young doctor would have a debt of about $85,000— representing the amount invested in his specialized training. This amount would be paid back with interest, and the total would be considered deductible from his income over the expected life of his practice. In a reasonably competitive environment, young people would then be able to make a free choice whether to pursue a medical career. Equilibrium in the number of doctors would be reached when the level of fees touched the point where the income, from medical practice, in excess of that of other occupations covered the normal return on the investment in professional training. *

Such a system may reduce the competitive level of medical fees. But more to the point, it would allow the supply of medical-training facilities to expand to meet the qualified demand. At the same time, it would remove the unwarranted public subsidy provided for medical (or other professional) training and return these funds to society for use elsewhere.

The details of the reforms in public finance could be argued. Nevertheless, the basic principles are clear. The first is that for tax purposes, incomes from all sources should be treated on an equal basis. The effective tax rates on income from property or capital should be the same as those imposed on the income derived from effort. (Note the adjective "effective." Although there is some attempt, in taxing property-derived income, to allow for depreciation and depletion of the capital base, nothing of the sort is done for earned income. Nevertheless, the income from human endeavor is not a permanent stream, but is attached to, and partakes of, all the hazards of the individual life. Some cognizance of this fact should be taken; but in fact the present tax codes tax the amortization of human capital as current income.)

On the expenditure side, there is a need to establish a limit on government expenditures at the level at which the public would be willing to pay the tax cost, assuming a full-employment level of national income. The provision of government services should be restricted to those where the element of interrelated common, or nonseparable utilities (or disutilities) is very strong. The budget

---

*In the early years of education and training, alternative occupations may pay more than medicine. This can be entered into the total net present-value calculation as a negative flow. Alternatively, the lost-opportunity earnings of this period could be considered as an addition to the total investment in training, for decision-making purposes (but not for tax purposes). Maintenance costs, food and lodging, do not enter into the problem since they would be incurred in any case.

makers need to use more restraint in drawing the line between public goods and those goods which may be provided as readily by the private sector. (Goods which may be bought by poor people are not necessarily public-sector goods. They may be provided by giving the poor money which will enable them to acquire their needs in the private sector.)

The last point of reform, which is much more difficult to implement than appears on reading, is to devise a poor-relief system that will provide a minimum acceptable income to the poor, with the following qualifications. The system must operate so that working always provides some net income over pure relief; so that there is always an income incentive for working. The system should be constructed so that there should be no incentive to move toward more expensive regions purely to increase welfare-income payments. (This means perhaps that the payments should be uniform throughout the country—with no regional cost-of-living adjustments.) Lastly, there should be no incentive to increase family size merely to supplement welfare income. This might mean that beyond a certain family size, benefits per child would decrease. Such a program is presently in effect in Singapore.

ACCOMMODATING SOCIETY TO A DISPARITY OF TALENTS

Early socialists presumed that talent was equally distributed and that different talents were equally in demand. Therefore, the sharp inequalities in the distribution of income were due to social inequities, such as exploitation, monopoly, racism, and other features of the capitalist system. The modern socialist has become more subtle. He argues, following Rawls, that the possession of talent is itself a matter of pure chance, and that thus the income derived from talent is akin to a pure economic rent that may well be taken away by society and redistributed to the less fortunate. Against this ideological position, one can only pose the counter philosophical argument that absolute income equality may not increase the sum total of human happiness. On an economic basis, absolute income equality will reduce allocative efficiency. Moreover, equal income would be very hard to enforce because there would always be arbitragers who could do well by doing good. They find ways of making money by shifting goods and services to those sectors of the economy where demand was higher. Such activities would always be rewarded by a profit.

Of course, there is a rear guard of socialists that still believes strongly that all human differences are a matter of training and environment. When it is shown that heredity seems to be a significant

factor in determining intelligence, and that intelligence roughly corre-
lates with income, they will argue that the most significant factor in
predicting income is the environmental influence of a good family.
The latter argument is circular; on examination, a good family back-
ground usually turns out to be strongly correlated with high-IQ parents.

At any rate, many recent works seem to imply that inherited
intelligence may have more to do with successful learning (or attain-
ment in a modern economy) than environmental factors. [12] Although
the evidence is not all in, the very thought is apparently disturbing;
because, to be fair, in practice, the doctrine of heredity has been
turned to some rather nasty uses. Thus, whereas the probability of
a genetic source of physical characteristics—strength, athletic coor-
dination, appearance, or musical or artistic talent—is generally
accepted, the idea that possibly individuals may be endowed with
different levels of learning ability is thought to be repugnant and is
simply not entertained by many socially sensitive people.

Nevertheless, the question that a libertarian might pose is
this. Suppose that the hypothesis that talents of all sorts, including
the talent for learning and for developing intellectual skills, are
largely inherent in the individual (not the tribe) is tentatively accepted.
Suppose that the ability to learn at all sorts of levels is innate. What
kind of society should be constructed? What social arrangements
would reasonably accommodate the facts of nature, the disparity in
inherited talents? What kind of economic and social framework, what
institutional arrangements would be fair and viable?

A basic framework can be derived from the values of liberal
tradition. However, because, for example, the basic value of personal equality, and that of recognizing and rewarding incentive and
achievement, may be somewhat in conflict, an absolutely ideal order-
ing does not seem possible. (But, of course, the willingness to enter-
tain the notion that some values may be in conflict is one of the
attractive features of the liberal tradition.) Moreover, even though
the weight given to various parts of the framework would be a matter
of individual taste and judgment, it does seem possible that a reasonably stable social consensus (which perhaps existed once) might be
developed around the following basic principles:

1. The fundamental premise of a libertarian, mobile society is
equality of opportunity. Opportunities for various types of training
and education must be open to every economic and social class. Equality of opportunity, however, does not guarantee equality of outcome.
Nor does equality of opportunity preclude the use of tests and quali-
fying examinations for establishing entrance to various professions
and positions where a minimal level of accomplishment is a public
desideratum.

The probability that intelligence is an inherent trait should lead to some modesty in forwarding claims for education as a device for achieving economic equality. The case for education as a producer good, a capital investment that increases lifetime income, has some merit, but it can be oversold. Much of education is similar to music and the arts; it should be considered a highly desirable consumption good that enhances the awareness and enjoyment of life. Basic education is on a slightly different footing, since it has an overwhelming public function in establishing a common base of discourse for the members of a society; beyond this point, education must be tailored to different talents.

2. The existence of variations in innate talents implies that final economic rewards may differ. Still, inequality of individual incomes should be moderated by a tax system that, at the very least, allows a basic exemption level of subsistence income.

3. The amount of wealth and power passed along by inheritance should be mitigated by inheritance taxes. Given a reasonable tax system and opportunities for economic and social mobility, inherited positions of power or wealth (unless the inheritors are natively skilled) will not be permanent over the longer run.

4. A system for providing a basic income for all families should be an automatic part of the public fisc. This system must not operate perversely so that incentives to work for additional income are dulled, or the production of large families is economically rewarding, or that socially expensive places or regions to live are preferred over relatively more reasonable areas.

5. It is very important that economic rewards and social recognition be given to a wide range of accomplishment. Athletic ability, good looks, endurance, faithfulness on the job, artistry, wit, good nature, mechanical skill—all these should be rewarded. Monetary awards and prizes might go to people in such categories as: best landscape artist of the year, most-skilled auto mechanic, best local driver, fastest and most-accurate checkout clerk, most-improved handball player, or best teacher. Perhaps sociologists could concentrate on creating devices to improve the reward system, instead of making surveys that encourage invidious comparisons.

6. There should be legal sanctions against arbitrary discrimination in initial hirings and promotions. The Chicago school of economics (Friedman et al.) argues that the best protection against discrimination is a truly competitive economic system. In such a system, the discriminators who refused to hire women or minority groups would bear the economic costs of their peculiar social preferences; they would have to pay more to obtain comparative skills and efficiency in their work force. In the long run, they would be driven out of business by more rational competitors. However, here

and now, we must recognize that portions of the private sector, and schools and governmental units do not operate in a fully competitive economy.

Nevertheless, laws in favor of fair employment practices must be administered with good sense. The charge of discrimination should be proven on a case-to-case basis (that is, by showing that qualified personnel were denied promotion on the arbitrary basis of race or sex). Discrimination cannot be proven solely by surveys showing the ratios of employment in different trades and professions, for various groups, since the assumption underlying such a survey is a gross aggregation that denies the possibility of variations in individual talents and proclivities.

The framework outlined above is obviously not complete. Moreover, if the model is to find a broad social acceptability, it needs some guiding institutions (in the Veblenian sense) of centrally held beliefs, values, and mores.

One may not need to go far into history to find the proper institutions. Tempered by the addition of some merely incremental amounts of tolerance, secularism, humanitarianism, racial respect, and internationalism, the professed ideals of the late nineteenth century and the first decade of the twentieth could furnish a start.

Specifically, society must restore the importance of work and recognize the value of workmanship. High marks should go to the honest workman-citizen who takes care of his obligations. Disregarding the Shavian beguilement, it would do no harm to reinstate the distinction between the deserving and the undeserving poor. Moreover, the use of the adjective "meaningful" in such expressions as "meaningful work" should be eschewed.

Because, unfortunately, differences in accomplishment often lead to jealousy, which may find an outlet in acts of violence, there is a need to relearn respect for the inviolability of the person and his immediate possessions. The sanction against violence should be observed with special force insofar as it concerns women, children, old people, scholars, judges, police, teachers, social workers, doctors, and clergymen; these people are either especially vulnerable in themselves, or their duties in society place them in vulnerable situations. *

-----

*From the evidence of the last two paragraphs, I fear that at the best I shall not fail to be accused of being a supporter of middle-class morality. However, it dawns on me that the use of "middle-class morality" as a pejorative term is of recent vintage. In fact,

The need for sanctions to protect teachers, social workers, doctors, and clergymen from violence is a pragmatic necessity, if they are to go out into the community and perform the task of making sure that the social environment affords an opportunity for health and talent to survive. The need for the physical safety of women, children, and old people is a matter of social morality akin to the provision of a minimum level of social security. The special plea for the protection of scholars derives from ethnic, religious, and social values and personal interest.

---

the liberal tradition is of middle-class origin. Moreover, the psychological importance of the work ethic and the instinct for workmanship can be found in writings as diverse as those of A. D. Gordon and Thorstein Veblen.

NOTES

1. Robert Heilbroner, Beyond Boom and Crash (New York: W. W. Norton, 1978), p. 85.

2. Irving Kristol, Two Cheers for Capitalism (New York: Basic Books, 1978), chaps. 30 and 31.

3. John Rawls, A Theory of Justice (Cambridge, Mass. : Harvard University Press, 1971).

4. Eli Schwartz, "The Cost of Capital and Investment Criteria in the Public Sector," Journal of Finance, March 1970.

5. See, for example, Marshall I. Goldman, The Spoils of Progress: Environmental Pollution in the Soviet Union (Cambridge, Mass. : MIT Press, 1972); see also, M. I. Goldman, "Growth and the Environmental Problems of Non-Capitalist Countries," in The Economic Growth Controversy, ed. Weintraub, Schwartz, Aronson (White Plains, N. Y. : 1973).

6. The data for the United States are from OECD, Energy Statistics (Paris: OECD).

7. J. Schumpeter, Capitalism, Socialism, and Democracy (New York: Harper and Brothers, 1947); also, H. Leibenstein, General X-Efficiency Theory and Economic Development (New York: Oxford University Press, 1978), p. 39.

8. E. Mishan, "Growth and Anti-Growth," in The Economic Growth Controversy, ed. Weintraub, Schwartz, Aronson, (White Plains, N. Y. : IASP 1973).

9. R. Aron, In Defense of Decadent Europe (Chicago: Regnery/ Galaway, 1979); reviewed by Stanley Hoffman, New York Times Book Review, June 17, 1979.

10. Kristol, op. cit. , pp. 265-70.

11. S. Freud, Civilization and Its Discontents (London: Hogarth Press, 1930).

12. For example, R. Hernstein, "I. Q. ," Atlantic Monthly, September 1971, and Arthur R. Jensen, "How Much Can We Boost I. Q. and Scholastic Achievement?" Harvard Educational Review, Winter 1969.

BIBLIOGRAPHY

Aldcroft, Derek H. , and Peter Fearon, eds. Economic Growth in Twentieth-Century Britain. London: Macmillan, 1969.

Allen, J. The British Disease. London: Institute of Economic Affairs, 1976.

Andersson, Ingvar. A History of Sweden. London: Weidenfeld and Nicolson, 1956.

Aron, Raymond. The Industrial Society. New York: Frederick A. Praeger, 1967.

Bacon, Robert, and Walter Eltis. Britain's Economic Problem: Too Few Producers. 2d ed. London: Macmillan, 1976.

Beckerman, Wilfred. Slow Growth in Britain. Oxford: Oxford University Press, 1979.

___. The British Economy in 1975. Cambridge: Cambridge University Press, 1965.

Boyd, Laslo V. Britain's Search for a Role. London: Saxon House; Lexington, Mass. : Lexington Books, 1975.

Brech, Ronald. Britain 1984: Unilever's Forecast. London: Darton, Longman & Todd, 1963.

Brittan, Samuel. The Economic Consequences of Democracy. London: Temple Smith, 1977.

Brittan, Samuel, and Peter Lilley. The Delusion of Incomes Policy. London: Temple Smith, 1977.

Cairncross, Sir Alec. Britain's Economic Prospects Reconsidered. Albany: State University of New York Press, 1970.

Caves, Richard E. , and Associates. Britain's Economic Prospects. Washington, D. C. : Brookings Institution; London: George Allen & Unwin, 1968.

Chickering, A. Lawrence, ed. The Politics of Planning. San Francisco: Institute for Contemporary Studies, 1976.

Childs, Marquis W. Sweden: The Middle Way. New Haven and London: Yale University Press, 1947.

Corden, W. M. , and Gerhard Fels. Public Assistance to Industry. London: Trade Policy Research Centre; Kiel: Institut für Weltwirtschaft, 1976.

Crosland, C. A. R. Britain's Economic Problem. London: Jonathan Cape, 1953.

Dahmen, Erik. Entrepreneurial Activity and the Development of Swedish Industry, 1919-39. Homewood, Ill. : Richard D. Irwin, 1970.

Deane, Phyllis, and W. A. Cole. British Economic Growth 1688-1959. Cambridge: Cambridge University Press, 1962.

Denison, Edward F. Why Growth Rates Differ: Postwar Experience in Nine Western Countries. Washington, D. C. : Brookings Institution, 1967.

Einzig, Paul. Decline and Fall—Britain's Crisis in the Sixties. London: Macmillan, 1969.

Freud, Sigmund. Civilization and Its Discontents. London: Hogarth Press, 1930.

Fry, J. A. Limits of the Welfare State—Critical Views of Post-war Sweden. London: Saxon House, 1979.

Geiger, Theodore, and F. M. Geiger. Welfare and Efficiency. Washington, D. C. : NPA Committee on Changing International Realities, 1978.

Gilbert, Milton, and Associates. Comparative National Products and Price Levels. Paris: Organization for European Economic Cooperation, 1957.

Gilbert, Milton, and Irving B. Kravis. An International Comparison of National Products and the Purchasing Power of Currencies. Paris: Organization for European Economic Cooperation, 1954.

Glyn, Andrew, and Bob Sutcliffe. Capitalism in Crisis. New York: Pantheon Books, 1972.

Glynn, Sean, and John Oxborrow. Interwar Britain. London: George Allen and Unwin, 1976.

Gruchy, Allan G. Comparative Economic Systems. Boston: Houghton Mifflin, 1966.

Hadley, Arkes. Bureaucracy: The Marshall Plan and the National Interest. Princeton: Princeton University Press, 1972.

Hansen, A. H. Full Recovery or Stagnation. New York: W. W. Norton, 1938.

Harris, Seymour E. Postwar Economic Problems. 1st ed. New York and London: McGraw-Hill, 1943.

Harrod, Roy. Are These Hardships Necessary? Rupert-Hart-Davis, 1947.

Hart, P. E. Studies in Profit, Business Saving and Investment in the United Kingdom. Vol. 2. London: Ruskin House, 1968.

Heclo, Hugh. Modern Social Politics in Britain and Sweden. New Haven: Yale University Press, 1974.

Heilbroner, Robert L. Beyond Boom and Crash. New York: W. W. Norton, 1978.

Hennessy, Josselyn, et al. Economic Miracles. London: Institute of Economic Affairs, Andre Denten, 1964.

Hudson Report. The United Kingdom in 1980. New York: Wiley, 1974.

Hutber, Patrick. The Decline and Fall of the Middle Class—and How It Can Fight Back. Harmondsworth: Penguin Books, 1977.

Jenkins, David. Sweden and the Price of Progress. New York: Coward-McCann, 1968.

Jewkes, John. Ordeal by Planning. London: Macmillan, 1946.

Kahn, Alfred E. Great Britain in the World Economy. New York: Columbia University Press, 1946.

Koblik, Steven. Sweden's Development from Poverty to Affluence, 1750-1970. Minneapolis: University of Minnesota Press, 1975.

Krause, Lawrence B. , and Walter S. Salant, eds. Worldwide Inflation. Washington, D. C.: Brookings Institution, 1977.

Krauss, Melvin B. The New Protectionism: The Welfare State and International Trade. New York: New York University Press, 1978.

Kravis, Irving B. , Alan Heston, and Robert Summers. International Comparisons of Real Product and Purchasing Power. Baltimore: Johns Hopkins University Press, 1978.

Kristol, Irving. Two Cheers for Capitalism. New York: Basic Books, 1978.

Kuznets, Simon. Economic Growth of Nations. Cambridge, Mass.: Harvard University Press, 1971.

Leibenstein, Harvey. General X-Efficiency Theory and Economic Development. New York: Oxford University Press, 1978.

Lieberman, Sima. The Growth of European Mixed Economies 1945-1970. New York: Schenkman Publishing Co. , 1977.

Lindbeck, Assar. Swedish Economic Policy. Berkeley: University of California Press, 1974.

Lundberg, Erik. Instability and Economic Growth. New Haven: Yale University Press, 1968.

Mathias, Peter, and M. M. Poston, eds. The Cambridge Economic History of Europe. Vol. 7. Cambridge: Cambridge University Press, 1978.

Meade, J. E. The Structure and Reform of Direct Taxation. London: George Allen and Unwin, 1968.

Mitchell, R. R. European Historical Statistics, 1750-1970. New York: Columbia University Press, 1975.

Morris, Derek. The Economic System in the U. K. London: Oxford University Press, 1977.

Nairn, Tom. The Break-up of Britain. Lowe & Brydonne Printers, 1977.

Nossiter, Bernard D. Britain— A Future That Works. Boston: Houghton Mifflin, 1978.

Oakley, Stewart. The Story of Sweden. London: Faber and Faber, 1966.

Okun, Arthur M. Equality and Efficiency: The Big Tradeoff. Washington, D C.: Brookings Institution, 1975.

Olson, Mancur. The Logic of Collective Action. Cambridge, Mass.: Harvard University Press, 1965.

Paish, F. W. Studies in an Inflationary Economy, The United Kingdom 1948-1961. London: Macmillan, 1966.

Postan, M. M. An Economic History of Western Europe 1945-1964. London: Methuen, 1967.

Prais, S. J. The Evolution of Giant Firms in Britain. Cambridge: Cambridge University Press, 1976.

Pratten, C. F. A Comparison of the Performance of Swedish and U.K. Companies. Cambridge: Cambridge University Press, 1976.

Robbins, Lionel. Aspects of Post-War Economic Policy. London: Institute of Economic Affairs, 1974.

Schnitzer, Martin. Income Distribution. New York: Praeger, 1974.

___. The Economy of Sweden. New York: Praeger, 1970.

Schumpeter, Joseph A. Capitalism, Socialism, and Democracy. 2d ed. New York: Harper and Brothers, 1947.

Shanks, Michael. Planning and Politics, The British Experience 1960-1976. George Allen & Unwin, 1977.

Shepherd, William G., et al. Public Enterprise: Economic Analysis of Theory and Practice. Lexington, Mass.: D. C. Heath, 1976.

Simons, Henry C. Economic Policy for A Free Society. Chicago: University of Chicago Press, 1948.

Stein, Bruno. Work and Welfare in Britain and the USA . New York: Wiley, 1976.

Tyrrell, Jr. , R. Emmett, ed. The Future That Doesn't Work. New York: Doubleday, 1977.

Weintraub, Schwartz, Aronson, eds. The Economic Growth Controversy. White Plains, N. Y. : IASP, 1973.

Weisbrod, Burton A. The Voluntary Nonprofit Sector. Lexington, Mass. : D. C. Heath, 1977.

White, T. H. In Search of History. New York: Harper and Row, 1978.

Wiles, P. J. D. Economic Institutions Compared. New York: Halsted Press, 1977.

Wiles, Peter. Krelle and Shorrocks, ed. Income Distribution. London: Institute of Economic Affairs, 1978.

INDEX

141

natural resource base: abuses of, 115; and economic growth, 5, 122; Sweden, U.K., and W. Germany compared, 6; Sweden and U.K., 69-70

New York City, analogy to U.K., 63

no-growth economy, 121, 122

nonmarket sector: in Sweden, 79; in U.K., 53, 54, 57

nuclear power and socialism, 114

occupational mobility, in Sweden, 75

Okun, Arthur, 7, 13

Olson, Mancur, 47, 64

organized labor, (see labor organization)

overmanning, 29, 46

Paish, F. W., 21

pension funds and capital market, 97

pensions, 82, 88, 103

performing arts, financing of, 117

Phillips, A. W., 91, 105

Phillips Curve, 58, 60, 91

Pigou effect, 51

Polk, Judd, 19

pollution and natural resources, 115, 122

population, growth, excess, 112

population of Sweden, 66: age structure, 83; homogeneity, 66

population mix, U.K., 66

pound, as reserve currency, 22

Pratton, C. F., 69, 105

price controls, U.K., 22, 24

price level changes: in Sweden, 91, 92; in U.K., 59

productivity, in U.K., 46, 47

profitability: in Sweden, 95, 97; in U.K., 39, 49

profits, decline of, in Marxist theory, 39, 108

profits in an open economy, potential in U.K., 23, 24

public finance reforms, 125

public goods: 53; financing of, 55; growth of, 57; problem with excess production, 52

rationalization of industry, 102

Rawls, John, 111, 131

real wages, 51, 102, 120

relief systems, 126, 129

return on capital, 61, 95, 96, 120

Robbins, Lord, 9, 13, 42, 60

Robinson, Joan, (Cambridge School), 69

Sadlowski-type unionization, 44

Samuelson, Paul A., 5, 13

savings, 98, 113

Saxons vs. Normans, 44

Say's Law, 9

Schumpeter, Joseph A., 9, 13, 66, 105, 131

Schwartz, Eli, 5, 131

scientific methodology, 106

Scimone, Guiseppe, 38, 64

Seers, D., 24

Shanks, Michael, 44, 64

shop stewards, in U.K., 43-44

Simons, Henry C., 28, 35

slow-growth economy, 121

Smith, Adam, 61

social contentment, 30, 40-42, 53, 110, 123-24

social goods, 52

social investments, optimum, 114

social security, in U.K., 30

social services, in Sweden: problem of costs, 68; transfer of income, 82

solidaristic wage policy, in Sweden, 74-75, 93

solidity (leverage), in Sweden, 95

ABOUT THE AUTHOR

ELI SCHWARTZ is the Charles MacFarlane Professor of Economics at Lehigh University, Bethlehem, Pennsylvania. He received an M.A. in economics from the University of Connecticut and a Ph.D. in economics from Brown University. He has written numerous books, monographs, and articles on economics.